IN THE NAME OF HUMANITY

Essayist, radio personality, journal editor and teacher, Alain Finkielkraut is one of France's leading intellectuals. He is the author of fourteen books, several of which have been translated into English, including *The Imaginary Jew*, *Remembering in Vain: The Klaus Barbie Trial*, and *The Defeat of the Mind*.

IN THE NAME OF HUMANITY

Reflections on the Twentieth Century

ALAIN FINKIELKRAUT

PIMLICO

Published by Pimlico 2001

2 4 6 8 10 9 7 5 3 1

First published in France as *L'Humanité perdue: Essai sur le xxe siècle* by
Editions du Seuil 1996
First published in the United States of America by
Columbia University Press 2000
First published in Great Britain by
Pimlico 2001

Pimlico
Random House, 20 Vauxhall Bridge Road,
London SW1V 2SA

Random House Australia (Pty) Limited
20 Alfred Street, Milsons Point, Sydney,
New South Wales 2061, Australia

Random House New Zealand Limited
18 Poland Road, Glenfield,
Auckland 10, New Zealand

Random House (Pty) Limited
Endulini, 5A Jubilee Road, Parktown 2193, South Africa

The Random House Group Limited Reg. No. 954009
www.randomhouse.co.uk

A CIP catalogue record for this book
is available from the British Library

ISBN 0-7126-6729-6

Papers used by Random House UK Limited are natural,
recyclable products made from wood grown in sustainable forests.
The manufacturing processes conform to the environmental
regulations of the country of origin.

Printed and bound in Great Britain by
Mackays of Chatham PLC

contents

translator's note

In translating *L'Humanité perdue*, I have taken the same liberty I did when translating *La Défaite de la pensée*, with quotations from works written orginally in French and other languages besides English. Whenever possible, I have provided the reader with references to published translations in English. Frequently, however, I have reworked the passages for stylistic purposes. Once again, I have remained faithful to the author's decision to use *man* and the male form of the third-person singular pronoun, even in contexts where Alain Finkielkraut is clearly speaking about both man and woman.

I would like to thank Mara Kolesas and, most especially, Timo Lyyra for their help in tracking down English translations of the many texts quoted in this book. In addition to the library work, Timo Lyyra kindly read an early draft of *In the Name of Humanity* and made a number of helpful suggestions. I am grateful as well to Richard Bernstein, Erwin Fleissner, Jerome Kohn, and Marta Petrusewicz for their assistance and advice. Alain Finkielkraut did me the great favor of reviewing early drafts of the translation.

IN THE NAME OF HUMANITY

The Last of the Just

TO QUALIFY IN AUSCHWITZ for Kommando 98, also known by the prisoners as the Chemistry Kommando, Primo Levi, a chemist, had to pass a special test. His examiner was Doktor Engineer Pannwitz:

Pannwitz is tall, thin and blond, with the kind of hair, eyes and nose that every German is supposed to have. He is seated menacingly behind an elaborate desk. And I, Häftling 174517, I stand in his office, which is a real office, neat and clean, with everything in order, feeling as if I would soil anything I touched.

When he finished writing, he raised his eyes and looked at me.

Since that day, I have thought about Doktor Pannwitz many times and in many different ways. I have often wondered about the inner workings of this man. What did he do with his time when he was not producing polymers in a chemistry lab, when he let his imagination wander beyond the reaches of Indo-Germanic consciousness? Above all, I wanted to meet him again, now that I was free, not out of revenge, but to satisfy my curiosity about the human soul.

Because the look he gave me was not the way one man looks at another. If I could fully explain the nature of that look—it was as if through the glass of an aquarium directed at some creature belonging to a different world—I would be able to explain the great madness of the Third Reich, down to its very core.

Everything we thought and said about the Germans took shape in that one moment. The brain commanding those blue eyes and manicured hands clearly said: "This thing standing before me obviously belongs to a species that must be eliminated. But with this particular example, it is worth making sure that he has nothing we can use before we get rid of him."[1]

To Doktor Pannwitz, the prisoner standing there, before the desk of his examiner, is not a frightened and miserable man. He is not a dangerous or inferior or loathsome man either, condemned to prison, torture, punishment, or death. He is, quite simply, not a man at all.

Gone are the days when a usurer, carrying all the sins of Israel on his back, might exclaim: "Hath not a Jew eyes? Hath not a Jew hands, organs, dimensions, senses, affections, passions? Fed with the same food, hurt with the same weapons, subject to the same diseases, healed by the same means, warmed and cooled by the same winter and summer, as a Christian is? If you prick us, do we not bleed? If you tickle us, do we not laugh? If you poison us, do we not die?"[2]

In the eyes of Doktor Pannwitz, Primo Levi sees the annihilation of the chosen people, the final end of any sense of species solidarity, which, for better or worse, used to recognize a bond between the vile Shylock and generous members of the human race. He whose name is Häftling 174517 can sob, bleed, smile, suffer, pass or fail a chemistry exam, but nothing changes the fact that an invisible wall, as watertight as the glass of an aquarium, will forever separate him from humanity. Exclusion, defamation, sarcasm, persecution, and massacre have existed for thousands of years, but now, swallowed up by silence in this totally impossible world that calls him a thing, the tirades, supplications, and complaints of all the Shylocks on earth cannot be heard. This is the great madness of the Third Reich.

No matter how insane it seems, this great madness is not the opposite of reason. Pannwitz has not lost touch with reality. He is not slipping. His perfectly functioning brain knows how to detect capable, educated, and performative qualities in waste material, identified as lowly vermin by Indo-Germanic science. With the aid of an aptitude test, Pannwitz measures the usefulness of the prisoner and then objectifies him even further. Instead of opening the doors of mutual recognition, the exam merely indicates whether vermin 174517 qualifies as exploitable waste material. If he does, Doktor Pannwitz will use him, provisionally, as part of the process that will lead to his eventual elimination.

Use him to make a profit. Liquidate him. The same industrial logic applies to both. The prisoner can be productive and noxious at the same time. Being competent is no argument for reintegrating him into the human species or even for sparing his life.

The man facing Häftling 174517 executes his task with the force of an intellect, both simple and formidable. Indifferent to the reasons why, the examiner cares only about the methodological and operational, responding with equal ease to every question that begins with *how*: How to make him contribute? How to kill him? How to use him? How to get rid of him? Against this absolute functionality, even usefulness does not help. In Doktor Pannwitz's soul, instrumental reason wins out over moral arguments, facts over common sense. This victory is the essence of his madness.

Interned in a lumber camp for Jewish soldiers captured during the "phony war," Emmanuel Lévinas was protected by his uniform from the fury of Nazi violence. His living conditions in the German forests had nothing in common with those endured by Primo Levi in Auschwitz. But he, too, felt like he was living in an aquarium:

> The other men, the ones we called free, who passed by or gave us work, or orders or even a smile—and the children and women who also passed by and occasionally looked at us—they all stripped us of our humanity. . . . With the strength and mis-

3

ery of the persecuted, a small inner voice, in spite of it all, re-called our fundamental essence as thinking human beings. But we were no longer part of the world.[3]

4

Then one day, for no apparent reason, a dog wandered into camp. The prisoners, dreaming of America and Americans, called the dog Bobby, and Bobby got into the habit of greeting them with a happy bark when they lined up in the morning and when they returned from work at night. "For him—without question—we were men." But this glimmer of reassurance could not last for very long: after a few weeks, the guards chased the troublesome animal out of camp, and the "last Kantian in Nazi Germany" continued on his meandering way.

Humanity, an idea forgotten by the rational animal, is remembered and reaffirmed by the noisy, puppy-dog effusions of a friend-ly beast deprived of "the brain power needed to universalize the great principles governing his drives."[4] Such is the dizzying origi-nality of the twentieth century, its unique contribution to the history of inhumanity.

one

Who Is Like Unto Me?

TO ACCEPT THE IDEA that all people in the world form a single humanity is not, it is true, the same thing as recognizing that they all belong to the human species. What distinguishes mankind from most other animals is precisely the fact *that he does not identify with others of his kind.* A cat for a cat has always been another cat. A man, on the other hand, must fulfill a set of Draconian conditions or be crossed off the list, without any recourse, of those counted as members of human society. From the very beginning, man jealously reserved the title of man for only those identified with his own community.

Must we therefore conclude that Pannwitz is the rule and not the exception? In a conference sponsored by UNESCO, almost six years after the unconditional surrender of a regime that valued people like Doktor Pannwitz, Claude Lévi-Strauss observed that

> the concept of an all inclusive humanity, which makes no distinction between races or cultures, appeared very late in the history of mankind and did not spread very widely across the globe. What is more, as proved by recent events, even in the one region where it seems most developed, it has not escaped periods of regression and ambiguity. For the majority of the human species, and for tens of thousands of years, the idea that humanity includes every human being on the face of the earth does not exist

at all. The designation stops at the border of each tribe, or linguistic group, sometimes even at the edge of a village. So common is the practice that many of the peoples we call primitive call themselves by a name which means "men" (or sometimes— shall we speak with more discretion?—the "good ones," the "excellent ones," the "fully complete ones"), thus implying that the other tribes, groups, and villages do not partake in human virtues or even human nature, but are, for the most part, "bad people," "nasty people," "land monkeys," or "lice eggs." They often go so far as to deprive the stranger of any connection to the real world at all by making him a "ghost" or an "apparition." Thus curious situations arise in which each interlocutor rejects the other as cruelly as he himself is rejected.[1]

It goes without saying that those who call themselves men know that they share basic physical similarities with other members of the species who come from elsewhere. If, nevertheless, they still give foreigners the names of insects or birds, it is because looking human is not enough. To belong to humanity, one must also practice certain specified customs dictated by the gods. In societies in which tradition reigns, there is, in other words, no place for the concept of tradition. Custom is sovereign because it is not seen as custom.

In societies like these, Shylock's tirade falls on deaf ears. His pathetic invocation of kinship among men, his desperate reference to shared reactions and drives, loses all power of persuasion. Having hands, organs, a body, senses, desires, and emotions; bleeding when pricked; laughing when tickled; taking revenge when hurt—these characteristics are perhaps universal, but they do not guarantee universal safe passage or even mutual recognition. What distinguishes some two-legged voluble creatures from others and allows them to join the community of humans is their way of life.

The Bible and philosophy gave our civilization the means to repudiate and challenge this widely held distinction between humans and nonhumans. To the people with whom he makes the covenant, to his dear beloved nation on whom he showers curses in ways unmatched by any other divinity, this God of the Bible declares: "The sentence you pass shall be the same whether it be on native or on stranger; for I am Yahweh your God."[2] The one God reveals to men the unity of humankind. An incredible message, an astounding revelation, which led Emmanuel Lévinas to say, "Monotheism is not an arithmetic of the divine. It is, perhaps, a gift from on high that makes it possible to see man's similarity to man beneath the continuing diversity of individual historical traditions."[3]

Beginning with a simple, big, and irreverent question—"What is?"—philosophy reveals the same truth as the Bible, but in an entirely different way. According to Goethe, "to be filled with a rush of emotion before the fantastic reality" that nothing said in the past predicts the future; to resist the answers handed down by the ancestors and think with unprecedented audacity about "what is truth, what is just, what is beautiful"; to say no longer, "this is good because it is our way" but to say instead, "where is the good so that we may serve it?" all this makes room within the self to look at the self from the outside. Customs that have ruled from time immemorial are suddenly open to comparison and judgment. For the first time, it is possible to distinguish the essential from the contingent, the natural from convention. Instead of experiencing it as truth, tradition becomes the subject of reflection. In the process of questioning the ways of the ancestors, an extraordinary concept emerges or allows itself to be seen, namely, the idea of a single humanity. That my customs follow one set of rules means that I could have had others without jeopardizing my membership to the human race. My humanity, in other words, is no longer tied to the way I do things. From this point on, I lose the right to judge those who act differently from me as unsuitable to bear the name of man.

With the rise of philosophy, truth freed itself from the chains of tradition: there was only one truth for all those not blinded by tradition. It sought a place for itself among all reasonable souls, everywhere and in every kind of climate. In the past, myths described what the gods had previously experienced. Now an emerging philosophy had replaced these stories, revealing a new passion for knowledge whose great project was the discovery of nature.

8   The nature uncovered and analyzed by philosophy was an *ordered* nature. Ancient cosmogony gave way to a magnificent cosmology. A hierarchical universe unveiled itself for serious study and took the place of the great origin myths, exposing a world to the objective observer with both high places and low:

> Below we find the theater of generational struggles and corruption of things that come from the four elements and return to them. Above reigns a fifth incorruptible element that moves in a circle, in keeping with its own nature. Below, events cannot repeat themselves exactly. The best they can do is create a cycle like the waters, the seasons, and animal species. But no one individual exists for eternity. Above, the stars are eternal. Below, everything flows like the current of a stream, every which way; above, "everything is pure orderliness and beauty."[4]

Thus the heavenly spheres are not only a space but also a model. In the splendor of the intangible, we discover something worth meditating on and knowledge worth acquiring. Making both physical and ethical demands, the heavenly hosts order man, the most noble of creatures living below, to raise his eyes and measure his actions by the stars. What the philosopher discovers when he looks at the universe is the visible image of perfection. In what then becomes known as philosophy, ontology is indistinguishable from axiology, and theory inseparable from the soul's yearning for grandeur.

Science in classical times was based on asceticism, not curiosity. Through intellectual work, it sought spiritual elevation. To understand the world according to truth is to understand it according to what is good; to know nature is to want to imitate it. And this imitation is possible only for those who make an effort to learn. As Plato said in *Timaeus*, one of his most influential texts:

It is only after having thoroughly studied the movements of the stars, after having acquired the power to calculate correctly in conformity with what occurs in nature, and after having imitated the movements of god, movements that absolutely never wander, will we be able to stabilize the movements in us that never stop roaming.[5]

The "movements in us that never stop roaming" are the impulses or drives of the body. To put ourselves in harmony with the admirable reign of tranquillity in the skies, we must subordinate the body to the rule of the soul, the affective or impressionable parts of our being to the rational parts. But people are endowed differently, and not all can achieve the same level of sovereign stability. Depending on the balance achieved between their earthly and heavenly parts, some men come closer than others to the natural model. As Aristotle concluded in a famous passage:

> All men who differ from others as much as the body differs from the soul, or an animal from man . . . are by nature slaves, and it is better for them, on the very same principle as in the other cases just mentioned, to be ruled by a master. A man is thus by nature a slave if he is capable of becoming (and this is also the reason why he actually becomes) the property of another and if he participates in reason to the extent of apprehending it in another though destitute of it in himself.[6]

In rejecting the multiplicity of traditions for the benefit of the ideal of an unconditional truth, philosophy creates a single world that is shared by all members of the human species, but the world it creates is vertical. And from a nature that is itself hierarchical, it deduces the natural hierarchy of men. The preeminence of the skies over the earth is thus reflected in the terrestrial relationship of superiors over inferiors. Implicated by *logos*, the idea of a universal humanity is held in check, or at least in respect, by cosmology.

Those living in the Middle Ages developed their worldview from the same cosmological system. While blaming the Jews for remaining stiff necked and headstrong in their particularism, St. Paul radicalized the biblical message and proclaimed, "There are no more distinctions between Jew and Greek, slave and free, male and female, but all of you are one in Christ Jesus,"[7] thereby paving the way for medieval theology to create a nonexclusive form of love for all members of the human race that was even more rigorous than the philosophy of the ancient Greeks. However, "Although original sin was replaced by the mercy of baptism for all the faithful," wrote Isidoro de Sevilla, "God, the righteous one, made distinctions between men, identifying some as slaves, others as masters, with the aim of giving the dominant ones the power necessary to discipline those who perform bad acts. For if there were no fear, how would it be possible to prevent evil?"[8]

All of humanity was corrupted by the Fall and redeemed by Salvation—this revelation of Christ's apostle yields, without resistance, before the divine vision of a ladder climbing up to Heaven, on which each individual takes his place according to his position in the hierarchy. Sin is unquestionably universal, as is Redemption, but this double universality does not disrupt the order of the world. On the contrary, it accommodates itself so obediently and with such docility that every hierarchical system is based on the assumption that there exists among creatures an unequal division between good and evil, the spirit and flesh, heaven and earth. It is because some creatures come closer to the holy that they devote themselves to the commandments or to spiritual life and because others, by nature, are base, almost integrally earthbound, that they find themselves condemned to perform tasks that satisfy bodily needs.

In sum, the Apostles and first philosophers may have solemnly proclaimed the unity of the human race in a society ruled by hierarchical principles, but men rarely believe they all belong to the same humanity. To use Tocqueville's elegant formulation, when differences are based on natural or divine assumptions, *one sees similarities only among members of one's own caste*. Thus in the ancient world among those who proclaimed universality, we see the following: "During their most enlightened period, the Romans used to tie the generals of their enemies to a chariot, drag them around triumphantly, then slit their throats, while they turned over lower ranking **11** prisoners of war to beasts of prey—all this for the amusement of the people."[9] And in the medieval world:

> When the chroniclers of the Middle Ages, all of whom belonged to the aristocracy by birth or education, recorded the tragic death of a nobleman, they described the last moments in painful detail, while on the same page they wrote about the massacre of humble people, without expressing any emotion.[10]

Continuing in the same vein, Ginés de Sepúlveda, a noted Spanish philosopher and church dignitary, made his famous argument in the great debate of Valladolid.

The year is 1550. It has been over half a century since the Spaniards established a foothold in America and the discoverers of the New World found themselves face-to-face with strange, unknown peoples. Nothing has prepared them for this, not the biblical account of creation, or the texts of the classical world, or any of the various encounters with otherness that Europe has previously experienced. Who are these feathered creatures? Do they deserve to be called men? Despite their exotic aspect, do they qualify as fellow human beings? Are they capable of reason? How should we treat them? Do they have a soul? Must we instruct them in the ways of Christianity, and if so, how? Once they become Christians, do we have the right to claim them as property?

Haunted by these questions, but not enough to keep Spain from using iron and fire in the New World, Charles V orders the suspension of all future conquests on April 16, 1550, and calls together a group of jurists and theologians to determine "how conquests may be conducted justly and in good conscience."[11]

Ginés de Sepúlveda and Bartolomé de Las Casas, "the great gatherer of Indian tears," give opposing views to the royal commission about whether the king can lawfully declare war on the Indians before preaching the faith to them. According to Sepúlveda, who opens the debate, there are four reasons justifying the declaration of war, making it both lawful and advisable:

> [1] The seriousness of the offenses committed by the Indians, particularly their idolatry and their sins against nature; [2] the coarseness of their intelligence, which makes them a servile and barbarous nation destined to be ruled by more advanced men like the Spaniards; [3] the needs of the faith, for their subjection will make preaching easier and faster; [4] the evil that they inflict on one another, killing innocent men to make sacrificial offerings.[12]

A remarkable scholar of ancient Greece, Sepúlveda has just translated Aristotle's *Politics*. Placing himself under the supreme authority of the philosopher, he uses Aristotle's logic to compare the conquerors with the natives, describing the former as examples of what the Greek philosopher meant by the rightful "domination of perfection over imperfection, strength over weakness, lofty virtue over vice."[13] The Indians, in contrast, Sepúlveda continues, indulge in all kinds of abominable passions. Before the Spaniards arrived, they waged war on one another with such ferocity that victory was useless and uninteresting if it did not allow them to satiate their appetites with the flesh of their enemies. The Scythians, observes the learned theologian, were also cannibals, but they were fearless warriors. As for the Indians, they are so cowardly that it usually takes only a few conquistadors to make them flee by the thousands, "like women." Thus whereas the Spaniards are prudent, brilliant, generous, temperate, pious and full of humanity, these little men (*homunculos illos*) have hardly a trace of humanity in them:

> Not only are they without science, but they do not use or know about any system of writing. They have preserved no historical monuments, except a vague and obscure memory of certain things recorded in a few paintings. Nor do they have

any written law; only a few barbaric rules and customs. They do not even recognize the right to own private property.[14]

Indians are as inferior to Europeans, Sepúlveda maintains, as children are to adults and women are to men. They are as different from Spaniards as the cruel are from the peaceful and as monkeys are from humans. How can anyone be surprised that such vile people, sullied with impurities and ungodliness, would be conquered by a nation filled with virtues? No matter how you look at it, the inhabitants of the West Indies fit the Aristotelian category of natural slaves. And if they reject the iron rule of their legitimate masters, the law commands that they be made to obey by the force of weapons.

Las Casas builds his argument on what seems to be the same philosophical ground. In response to the idea that it is legitimate and necessary to enslave people who have neither faith nor law, the bishop of Chiapas describes the Indians as having well-established customs and a disciplined way of life. Since Aristotle is the point of reference, Las Casas uses the Greek philosopher against his opponent and demonstrates with powerful examples that the people of the New World give evidence of being prudent, that is, of having the aptitude to govern—in their individual behavior and in the way they organize their families, their communities, and even their cities and kingdoms. *Prudencia monástica, prudencia económica, prudencia política.* Eminently reasonable, civilized, and evolved, those whom we call the Natural Ones fulfill all the conditions outlined by Aristotle for determining who should attain the good life.

The bishop's demonstration of Aristotelian orthodoxy is a rhetorical exercise, not a pledge of allegiance. In no way does it challenge the fact that Sepúlveda and Las Casas see the world differently. One still inhabits the cosmos, while the other has abandoned the conception of a universe with ontologically distinct elements. According to the apologist of the conquest, nature is based on the principle of inequality, with recognized ranks, grades, hierarchical levels, and orders. For the defender of the Indians, the same law governs a unified space and a homogeneous reality. As he now sees the world—the bishop's thoughts on the matter having changed after he lived in Mexico—the very idea of a natural slave is unacceptable. Nature is what unites men; it does not separate them.

14   Let Shylock hold his head high. Nowhere on earth can human beings rightfully be excluded from mankind or assigned according to their nature or needs to the supervision of others. For "everyone delights in the good and feels pleasure in what is agreeable. Everyone hates evil and flees from it, experiencing discomfort in what is unpleasant and bad."[15]

In making his case, however, Las Casas does not draw on the philosophical tradition of Naturalism. He takes no satisfaction in challenging the arrogance of the Aristotelian system of classification with a few simple, modest, fundamental, and universal drives. He would never reduce customs in all their diversity to a schema that identified common needs. People in every culture may seek ways to feel good, flee evil, and avoid being uncomfortable, but these similarities do not come close to explaining what makes particular groups or individuals human.

What is more, placing human beings in a grand universal scheme, subjecting them all to the same basic laws that govern life, does not deny the inner presence of an ideal. Big upheavals in the physical world affect the spiritual world as well. If everything is now on the same level, if the distinction between high and low is no longer important, then no one can use his individual position for personal gain. If there is no single place for God, then all places are equidistant from the heavenly source. One group of people is no closer or farther away than another. A similar sense of nostalgia, a similar desire to bridge the unattainable distance, will lead all human beings in their different ways to honor the eternal and to call out the divine name.

No matter what rituals are performed, the same dedication and devotion are at work. Communicating with the invisible one is no longer the personal privilege of a particular group or class. No single belief has a monopoly on the true faith. Truth is one, as it must be, but it can no longer be easily recognized. Instead, it creeps in between unity and diversity, establishing a relationship between the two that is without precedent. It is no longer error, but truth that manifests itself in many ways; the very multiplicity of forms of religious belief demonstrates the universality of religion. Tolerance as a value evolves out of "delocalization," that is, out of liberating the Holy One from one particular place.

Before Galileo and the sanctioning of science, Nicholas Cusanus pushed this egalitarian cosmology to its theological and moral limits in *De docta ignorantia* and *De pace fidei*.[16] Influenced by Cusanus, the great defender of the Indians used his perception of an egalitarian cosmology to redefine the very meaning of the evangelical mission and to support vigorously the right, even obligation, of the pagans to defend their idols: "Since the idolaters assume that their idols are the true God, they address themselves and direct their beliefs towards the true God."[17]

Two languages, two worlds. When the debate finally ended, the judges of Valladolid refused to favor one position over the other. After pitting the champion of the conquerors against the self-declared enemy of the conquest, the doctrinal conflict was left unresolved. Sepúlveda wrote to a friend that with the exception of one theologian, the judges concluded it was legitimate for the Christians to dominate the barbarians of the New World. Las Casas claimed that the assembly had ruled in his favor but that "unfortunately for the Indians the measures decreed by the council were not well executed."[18]

Whom should we believe? We know the Crown never endorsed the bellicose writings of Sepúlveda, but we also know that the municipal council of Mexico voted to give him gifts of clothing and jewels as a way of expressing their admiration and gratitude. We cannot ignore the fact, either, that Philip II did not improve the lot of the Indians. A few years after the controversy, when the king published a new ordinance to regulate recent discoveries and future exploits on land and on sea, he merely substituted the term *pacification* for *conquest*.

Still, it is also true that Las Casas succeeded in changing the meaning of the word *barbarism*. And in doing so, he opened up a subversive new field of inquiry that continues to thrive to the present day. The defender of the Indians placed those who stubbornly held on to a hierarchical vision of humanity at the bottom of the ladder. In his eyes, they were fooled by custom and appearance: those who claim they can recognize a monk by his habit are only showing that they lack education and are insensitive and coarse. When people let money define status, he argued, they demonstrate the narrowness of their spirit and the primitiveness of their nature.

The confrontation with the Americas inspired a new and great European concept: *barbarian Europe*, the idea of an obtuse civilization in which "the one who says it is it!" Thus Las Casas noted in his *Apologética historia*: "We consider a people barbarian when they do not have a system of writing or a scholarly language. But the people of the Indies could treat us as barbarians, since we do not understand their language."[19] During the same period, Montaigne observed in the *Essays*:

> From what I have heard, there is nothing barbarian or savage in these people, except that everyone calls barbarian that which he does not do himself; it seems that we have no other measure of truth and reason than the beliefs and customs of the country from which we come. Our religion is always perfect, the police is perfect, everything we do is done to perfection.[20]

The same idea inspired Montesquieu two centuries later to use bitter irony in ridiculing the case made for enslaving black people: "These creatures are black from head to toe; and their noses so flat that it is impossible to feel sorry for them. One cannot imagine that God, who is a very wise being, put a soul, especially a good soul, in a body so completely black."[21] And Lévi-Strauss—the last of the great inheritors to date of this beautiful tradition—gave his most forceful formulation in a lecture prepared for UNESCO: "The barbarian is first and foremost a man who believes in barbarism."[22]

How about the man who believes in the intrinsic superiority of the upper classes? The man who sees in the rules of protocol the divine order of things? The one who confuses personage with person and who, identifying heavenly design with pomp and circumstance, feels a sense of religious respect before the ostentatious display of nobles, the magnificence of the Church and the vanities of power? This man **17** is certainly less disagreeable than the civilized barbarian described and ridiculed by Las Casas, Montaigne, Montesquieu, and Lévi-Strauss; for instead of excluding the Other from the category human, he excludes himself from an ideal, all-encompassing, humanity. Never, as Groucho Marx used to say, would he belong to a club that would accept him as a member.

What is more, the same individual can hold both positions at once, for a similar mechanism is at work, inspiring the humility of "inferiors" and the haughtiness of conquerors. Pascal was the first to demonstrate this: in a world deserted by the divine voice, where only "eternal silence" is heard, it is by virtue of the imagination alone, "this mistress of error and duplicity," that differences of rank among men acquire a metaphysical dimension. "Who hands out reputations? Who apportions respect and veneration to people [What gives values to] achievements and laws . . . if not this faculty of imagination? All the wealth of the world would be insufficient without its help."[23]

When the world is a cosmos, the hierarchical principle inscribes itself on the order of things. But when Heaven stops serving as a protective cover, the supernatural loses touch with human experience and relies instead on the realm of illusion. The obvious turns into a trap, and the earthly manifestation of the divine becomes a grandiose fiction, replete with special effects. Credulity, not faith, holds up the social structure. Artifice now reigns where the eternal one ruled previously, and mirage takes the place of miracle. As the all-powerful departs, he cedes the splendor of truth to the empire of false representations; the divine comedy makes way for the great human comedy: "Our magistrates understood the power of mystery well. Their red robes, their ermine capes, in which they wrapped themselves like furry cats, the courts where they sat, the *fleurs de lis*, they knew they needed all these august trappings."[24]

With fierce passion, Pascal made sure that nothing remained in the religion he professed of the belief in the divine origin of the social order: "The title by which you possess your goods is not a title bequeathed by nature, but a human institution," he wrote, dismissing men in high places who allow themselves to believe the superstitious reasons given for why they hold positions of authority above common men. There are many different social conditions but only one human condition, Pascal continued as he pursued his relentless campaign against the aristocracy's self-serving assumptions about their God-given rights: "Your body and soul are indifferent to your station in life, be you a barge man or duke; no natural bond ties you to one social position or another."[25]

After making the case against it, Pascal went on to praise mystification. People believe in all this political and social witchcraft. Despite the abuse, they blindly accept lavish displays of authority, privilege, and power. What is more, to open their eyes and turn them away from their error would be a terrible mistake. They are right to be wrong, and their madness or naïveté is much wiser than the insight they would gain by following the teachings of so-called experts "who disturb the world and make negative judgments about everything," calling out their truth from the rooftops.

Everybody wants to rule over everyone else and is therefore everyone's enemy. The only alternative for hierarchy and pretense is the terror of civil war. Imagination, with all its drawbacks, keeps the peace by putting intelligence to sleep. It tranquilizes the desire for glory, calms feelings tormented by envy and the passion to dominate. Imagination, in other words, dulls the first and worst form of concupiscence: self-love.

Let sleeping egos lie. This negative certainty forces those who understand it to continue playing the game and join the multitudes in bowing down before displays of grandeur. Avoiding cries of suspicion, they do not reveal the secret that all men are equal. Thus Pascal, with all his cleverness, did his part, unexpectedly, to help fool the fools.

In the end, despite attempts to dissemble his actions, Pascal's intervention was a form of defection. He might have put back the mask of rank and class on all the faces he had cruelly uncovered. He might have accepted the great political and social lie as the imperfection of human nature or the curse of God, recognizing that it had weighed heavily on humanity since the time of the Fall. But these gestures of his were all in vain. The damage had been done; his heart was no longer in it. No matter how hard he tried to deny it, his work contributed to the demystification of the social order and would lead men to live inequality differently. In *Pensées*, Pascal outlined step-by-step the democratic transformation of unequal relationships. His later recommendation to be hypocritical merely marked the end of innocence, revealing a world now informed, one in which, as Tocqueville lucidly wrote, "It is in vain that wealth and poverty, authority and obedience, accidentally create great distances between two men[:] public opinion founded upon the usual order of things, levels the distances and creates a kind of imaginary equality between people, despite the real inequality of their social conditions."[26] Thus, imaginary equality dethroned the fantasy of inequality among men, introducing the idea of the "ulterior motive," which, like a worm in a piece of fruit, eats away at societies based on hierarchical principles while also rotting to the core those based on individual equality.

But do individuals always have ulterior motives for their actions? A century after Pascal, Enlightenment philosophers took pleasure in seeing the secret held only by specialists abandon the mind, take up residence in the body, and become common sense. The clarity of the spirit is unexpectedly confirmed through the tears of the body, through what the philosophers joyously called *human feelings*: "This noble and sublime enthusiasm," wrote Diderot in the *Encyclopaedia*, "is tortured by the sufferings of others and by the need to soothe them; it wants to travel all over the earth abolishing slavery, superstition, vice, and unhappiness."[27] Thus, by following Pascal and taking his ideas to their logical conclusion, the encyclopédistes, with Voltaire, were able to defend humanity against this "sublime misanthrope": the self, they maintained, is not hateful, or no longer is, for man is compassionate.

The new paradigm used for defining human relations set the stage for the coming revolution, which announced itself by calling for "the sensitive recognition of man by man."[28] In order to prove that all men are the same required demonstrating man's unlimited capacity for sympathy and for identifying with all the suffering that strikes the human species. The democratic man who emerges in the process has lost his innocence but gained feelings. His sense of sympathy increases as his respect for hierarchy decreases: the less bedazzled, the more tender; the less deferential, the more impressionable; the less obsequious, the more forgiving. It is because he laughs with such insolence that the mischievous Figaro, immune to all forms of idolatry, can cry so prodigiously. His ability to commiserate increases at the same rate as his sense of equality; his heart develops its own reason that reason itself corroborates. "Are we more sensitive than our fathers?" asked Tocqueville, the great anthropologist of this historical transformation. Yielding to a rush of natural enthusiasm, he answered:

> I do not know, but what is absolutely clear is that we are sensitive to many more things. When a people are all almost equal in rank, they have, more or less, the same way of thinking and feeling. Each one can judge in a minute what all the others are experiencing. He looks quickly at himself; that is all he has to do. He cannot, in other words, conceive of any misery without feeling pain, the extent of which is revealed to him through a secret instinct. Even when it involves strangers or enemies, it is to no avail; his imagination puts him in their place, mixing something personal with his pity, making him suffer while he watches [his side] tear apart the body of his fellow being.[29]

To no avail: Tocqueville had already used this phrase when speaking about the division of society into classes. Here again he uses it to mark the defeat of difference before sameness. Imagination, which earlier recognized the differences between one man and another is now climbing over the widest walls, seeping into every symbolic and geographic crack that might divide humanity. Under the influence of this new form of coexistence—of the rising equality of conditions—one's fellow man becomes everybody and anybody, even if he is a foreigner or an enemy.

The Italian officer Emilio Lussu described how the idea of an enemy failed to hide the common bond that men feel for one another. On a calm clear night in September 1916, he had an unexpected and disconcerting experience. Fighting at the time on the Asiago Plateau, he ventured out of his trench with another soldier to try to spot the invisible cannon that had been shooting at his men for several days. After crawling a few yards, he reached a place where by chance he could spy on the enemy, lined up in their trenches, all in a row. What he saw was strangely familiar:

> There they were these Austrians, so nearby that we could almost touch them, just as peaceful as people walking along, on a city street. . . . An unknown life unfolded before our eyes. We had come to see these trenches, which we attacked so often and with no success, as places with no life, gloomy, abandoned of anything living, a refuge for mysterious and terrible things. . . . Now the trenches revealed themselves as they truly were. The enemy, the enemy, the Austrians, the Austrians! . . . This was the enemy and they were Austrians. Men, soldiers like us, made like us, in uniforms like us, who were moving, speaking, drinking their coffee, exactly as our own men were doing at the very same hour. How strange. Such an idea had never occurred to me. They were drinking coffee now. But why was I so surprised by the fact that they were drinking coffee? Around 10:00 or 11:00 they would have their soup, just like us. After all, could the enemy live without drinking and eating? Certainly not, so why was I amazed?[30]

Although he went out to find the enemy, Emilio Lussu encountered soldiers like himself. Of course, he learned nothing he did not already know. He did not need to verify that the Austrians were men.

Believing in the war, he had wanted to do his part to prevent the Central Powers from winning a military victory. He had also wanted to challenge the forces of reaction gaining in Italy and throughout all of Europe. But he never once thought he was fighting against members of another species. Propaganda was a disease of the home front; it did not affect him.

Still, he was fighting the enemy, and much to his amazement, upon seeing them up close, he suddenly felt a sense of community that until then, the war had eclipsed. There was now a crack in his armor, and Shylock's protestations were seeping through. As if this were not enough, more surprises were in store for him.

Suddenly, an officer arrived. The Austrian soldiers stopped talking and drew apart, making room for their commander to pass by. Lussu, who had been in the war for a long time and had developed the mindset of a warrior, took the rifle from the corporal who was accompanying him. He said to himself that after waiting for so many hours, after so many patrolling parties, so much lost sleep, it would be madness to let this big game slip away, just as he came within range. But a simple gesture turned him from his violent intentions:

The Austrian officer lit a cigarette. Now he was smoking. This cigarette formed an invisible bond between us. No sooner did I see the smoke than I wanted a cigarette myself, which reminded me that I had some with me. But that lasted only a minute. I became conscious of my automatic, mechanical act of aiming my weapon and aiming it at somebody. My index finger, which was touching the trigger, relaxed. I began to think. I was forced to think. . . .

Maybe it was the total calmness that turned my thoughts away from war. Facing me was a young officer who was unconscious of the danger threatening him. I could not possibly miss hitting him. I could have fired a thousand rounds from this distance and never missed a single shot. All I had to do was pull the trigger and he would have fallen to the ground. Knowing that his life depended entirely on what I

decided to do made me hesitate. A man was standing before
me, a man.

A man!

I could see his face perfectly, even the whites of his eyes. **23**
Dawn was rising, making it easier to see everything, and the
sun was coming up from behind the mountains. How could I
shoot a man standing only a few feet away, just like that . . . as
if he were a wild boar?[31]

At the very moment he prepared himself to do what was in his best
interest—what his conscience ordered and what his many years of experience in war told him to do—Lussu was struck down by the evidence, as if it were a bolt of lightning. A shadow separated itself from
the officer's body. The trivial gesture of lighting a cigarette, this seemingly insignificant detail, stripped the enemy of two qualities: of being
an officer and of being an enemy. Losing the visible determinations of
his being, what was suddenly left bare was his abstract form, independent of status, function, and rank—his very humanity: "A man
was standing before me!" This confusing discovery was no reflection
on the quality of Lussu's mind but on the workings of his imagination.
Recognizing their common humanity, Lussu put himself in the place
of the unknown person whom he held in his power. Without warning, pity overwhelmed him. In this case, pity meant not only repug-
nance at seeing someone like himself suffer (following Rousseau's famous definition), but also identification with the deadly suffering that
he was preparing to inflict. He was one, and now, unintentionally, he
was two. The sniper felt his target's pain; the hunter suffered for his
prey. In a matter of minutes, the irresistible force of empathy transformed the scrupulous soldier. This "melting and sudden collapse of
his autistic disposition"[32] made him temporarily incapable of performing his military obligation. Unable to get hold of himself, to stop
this emotional response, Lussu, weary of war, offered the rifle to the
corporal. But he too was suffering from the same imaginary hemor-
rhage, paralyzed by the same evidence, and refused to take the weapon. And so they crawled back to their trench, empty-handed.

This little episode does not shield us from any of the horror of World War I. It only teaches us that the terrible massacre of those years did not completely destroy human ties between men. Doktor Pannwitz, in contrast, would never have reacted this way. For him, there was no possibility of identifying with the prisoner trembling with fear before his immaculate desk. He could not see him up close. No mixing with the riffraff in his imagination, no split personality threatening his physical or mental well-being.

It goes without saying that Pannwitz and his peers are not exceptional cases. For as both Lévi-Strauss and Tocqueville have shown, recognition between men is the product of history. It is far from being natural among all human beings. But remembering this does not explain the mystery of the twentieth century; it only makes it all the more difficult to understand. How is it possible that after recognizing the bonds existing between men that so many men could end up on the other side of the divide, merely by virtue of a decree proclaimed by other men? How could they calmly accept a philosophy of violence far greater than anything espoused by the people Lévi-Strauss writes about? How was it possible for the concept of universal humanity to fall into such massive and radical oblivion in the center of the very civilization where it reached its most spectacular development? Is regression, the term Lévi-Strauss has used for it, adequate to describe this enigma?

two

The Glamorous Appeal of the
Common Noun

IN *THE COMMITTED OBSERVER*, Raymond Aron recalled a conversation he had with Sartre in 1945 about the cool reception France gave to the Jews who survived deportation and returned home from the camps: "We asked ourselves: Why was there not a single article, not even one, saying, 'Jews, welcome home, welcome back into the French community.' Was the real reason for silence that the French had something to hide?"[1] Eager to rebuild their image through the experiences of those who had opposed Vichy, to see themselves as a people engaged in resistance, the French told other stories about the war and avoided remembering the extermination camps.

Sartre broke the silence in 1946 with the publication of *Anti-Semite and Jew*. Taking it upon himself to speak for the French, he welcomed the Jews home. Without mentioning the genocide directly, the extent of which was still not known in the months immediately following the war, Sartre's short, tightly argued book made it difficult to act "as if it [anti-Semitism] were unimportant." At the very moment when France was trying to finesse the matter, in part out of exhaustion, Sartre picked up his pen and produced his magisterial and devastating portrait: "The phrase, 'I hate the Jews,' is one that is uttered in chorus; in pronouncing it, one attaches himself to a tradition and community—the tradition and community of the mediocre."

We must remember that a man is not necessarily humble or even modest because he has consented to mediocrity. On the contrary, there is a sense of passionate pride among the mediocre, and anti-Semitism is an attempt to give value to mediocrity as such, to create an elite of the ordinary. A little further on, Sartre is more specific:

> By treating the Jew as an inferior and pernicious being, I affirm at the same time that I belong to the elite. In contrast to most modern elites, which are based on merit or labor, this elite closely resembles that of an aristocracy determined by birth. There is nothing I have to do to merit my superiority, nor is there anything I can do to lose it. It is given once and for all. It is a *thing*.[2]

In other words, for Sartre the anti-Semite yearns for a vertical social order. Disenchanted with the world, he deplores the disappearance of a time when society had visible social classes and a natural hierarchy. Confronted with the abyss of uncertainty where the concept of fellow man threatens to embrace all of humanity, he pulls back in fear, expressing a desire to see everything in its place, the way it used to be, when one's essence was determined by birth. The anti-Semite needs the Jew in order to identify himself as the rightful heir and to escape the worries and torments of a purely individual existence.

If men are first and foremost men and only afterward members of a caste or aristocratic lineage, then they no longer belong to what they belong. When man cannot be reduced to his rank, position, community, nation, ethnicity, or lineage, this is freedom. And that is why there is something undesirable about freedom. The anti-Semite has proved it. The privilege gained is constraining and painful. The gift of freedom is no gift at all: nothing is given away anymore. With freedom, everyone becomes accountable for his destiny.

More than anything else, the anti-Semite wants to undo this difficult obligation. As Sartre put it:

> He is afraid, not of the Jews, to be sure, but of himself, of his own consciousness, of his freedom, of his instincts, of his re-

sponsibilities, of being alone, of change, of society and the world—of everything but the Jews. . . . In espousing anti-Semitism, he does not simply adopt an opinion, he chooses himself as a person. He chooses the permanence and impenetrability of stone, the total irresponsibility of the warrior who obeys his leaders—and he has no leader. He chooses to acquire nothing, to deserve nothing; he assumes that everything is given to him as a birthright—and he is not of the nobility. He chooses finally a Good that is ready-made, beyond question, out of reach; he dares not examine it for fear of being led to challenge it and having to seek another. The Jew only serves as a pretext; elsewhere his counterpart will use the Negro or the man with yellow skin.[3]

Thus, although many see anti-Semitism as one form of racism among others, Sartre sees racial hatred beginning with a hatred of Jews. What is more, the Jew, the black man, and the man with yellow skin are all victims of the same revolt against the growing popularity of the idea of fellow man and its irresistible universalization. In every case, the revolt calls for a return to that blessed time when origins had the force of law. But since medieval theology and ancient cosmology were scientifically disqualified, it is through science and the field of biology that the desire for preeminence and immunity is now preserved. Since there no longer is a higher world or supernatural order to explain the disparities among men, we must look for answers in the inherited physical characteristics of different human groups—on this side of consciousness and the person, not on that other metaphysical side. At that very moment when the holy one disappears without leaving an address, genetic determinism arrives to take his place, ensuring the ongoing inequality among races, the unequal division between body and spirit, the material and the ideal.

This is a "soft kind of Humanism," a redundant formulation recently introduced by Michel Foucault. "Humanism," he stated, "implies softness." Foucault then explained that this provocative, singular, and mysterious description allowed him to understand the meaning often given to the death of man: "You cannot imagine the moralizing swamp of humanistic sermons we wallowed in after the war. Everyone was a humanist. Camus, Sartre, Garaudy, they were all humanists. Stalin too was a humanist."[4]

Foucault's summary attack is both scathing and unfair. What is unacceptable about it is not only the way it mixes together, or associates with one another—a satrap, an imbecile, and two writers—but also the way it depicts the postwar period as edifying and moralizing when it was above all a traumatized time. Foucault's irony seems to forget what war this postwar period followed. The dominant mood was not one of preaching but of horror. The scales tilted toward humanism not out of complacency before the great achievements of mankind but astonishment and panic before the temptation of acting in an inhuman way. This humanism had nothing to do with those who sang praises of *Homo sapiens*, *Homo faber*, *Homo loquax*, the rational animal, or with those who compared the excellence of our being or the innocence of our nature with different varieties of the ascetic ideal. This humanism, tormented by the war, did not ask how it might reconcile itself with human beings who had been demeaned and slandered far too long by religious morality. It asked an entirely different question: how does man acquire the desire to rid himself of his humanity? What is there in the humanity of man that is so unbearable and, at the same time, so fragile?

Sartre clarified the matter in a lecture entitled "Existentialism Is a Humanism," delivered in Paris on October 29, 1945, to a packed and highly charged house. Determined to answer the criticisms that his work had already provoked and to dispel any misunderstandings, Sartre decided to be didactic. He began, therefore, with the most prosaic reality of everyday life:

> When one looks at a manufactured object, for example, a knife used for cutting the pages of a book, it is an object made by an artisan who had a previous idea of what it would be. In making it, the artisan had in mind the concept of a particular kind

of knife and of a preexisting technology for making it, which is also part of the conception and which is, in the end, the blueprint for producing it. And so, the knife is an object that is made in a certain way for a defined purpose. It is impossible to imagine that a man would produce a knife to cut the pages of a book without knowing beforehand what it would be used for. Thus we can say that for the knife, its essence, that is, the blueprint and qualities that make it possible to produce and define, precedes its existence.[5]

Then, Sartre continued, the difference between man and a knife made for cutting the pages of a book is that there is no conception of man such that each individual could be an identical copy. Man is not produced; he is born. He is not the result of a preexisting idea but the ordinary miracle of a pure beginning. In other words, man is a being in which existence precedes essence.

What do we mean by saying that existence precedes essence? We mean that man exists first, suddenly appears in the world, then encounters himself and defines himself afterwards. If man, as the existentialist sees him, is not definable, it is because in the beginning he is nothing. He will only be something later on and only what he makes of himself. Thus there is no human nature, for there is no God to have a conception of it.[6]

Existentialism: the word is new, but the definition of it is not. Imagining God with the characteristics of an all-powerful creator, Sartre tears man away from the grip of the divine. Yet in a founding work of humanism, the famous *De dignitate hominis*, composed in 1486 by Giovanni Pico della Mirandola, it was God himself who suspended the universal law of creation for man. Beginning with a myth, Pico della Mirandola explained that man was the result of an improvident or distracted demiurge. After having created the world according to the ways of his impenetrable wisdom, the sovereign architect did not want to remain alone before his magnificent achievement. He needed an admirer, a being who would absolutely understand the reason for his work and would love it for its beauty. He dreamed, therefore, of producing mankind. The universe, however, was already filled with creatures. There were no prototypes in stock; they had all been given away. The perfect craftsman lacked concepts and models. Nevertheless, he was determined to succeed. God "finally decided that to the one to whom he could give nothing that would be uniquely his own, he would give everything that had been given to every other creature." He thus took man—this piece of work that had no distinct image— and placing him in the middle of the world, God sent him on his way with these words:

> I gave you no particular place, face, or talent. Whatever you want you must conquer and take possession of by yourself. Nature limits other species by the laws I established. But you, closed in by nothing, have the ability to make decisions about things placed in your own hands by me. You define who you are by yourself. . . . I made you neither celestial nor terrestrial, neither mortal nor immortal, so that, ruler of yourself, you will freely finish the work of determining your final form as would a painter or sculptor. You can degenerate into lower forms, like those of the beasts or, regenerated, reach up to higher forms that are divine.[7]

Sartre's proposition "existentialism is a humanism" is therefore not at all paradoxical. In fact, the original humanism is itself an existentialism insofar as it shields man from all conceptual strictures. What distinguishes Sartre from the Renaissance philosopher is not so much the content of his thought as the disposition of his soul. Pico della Mirandola's discourse on the dignity of man bears good news: "Everything is possible" for those whom tradition has wanted to contain—between angel and beast—in an already determined existence. Each being is what it is by its nature, except man. Man is the exception among creatures. Nothing stands in his way. Instead of inheriting his life completely defined by the order of things, man has the power to give his life form; such is his greatness and dignity.

With Sartre, the tone of the message changes radically. There is no expansive promise in his discourse. Instead, he lays bare an inescapable condition: man is destined to be free. And he does not always enjoy it! The proof? Man dreams about giving up the privilege. **31** By every means possible, he tries to get rid of the inconvenient gift he received from the dizzy God of Pico della Mirandola.

In *Being and Nothingness*, Sartre described in meticulous detail the many methods and tricks available to man to ensure that his dream of giving up freedom would come true. With unrelenting skill, Sartre continued where Pascal left off. First, Pascal reminded mortals who lived within their useful but specious hierarchical order of an equally corrupted natural order and of a final act that would necessarily be bloody, "no matter how beautiful the rest of the play might have been." Now Sartre questioned the solidity of this nature and used all his ingenuity to describe the *Comedy of Being*. What, therefore, is the waiter in a café doing "when he approaches customers just a little too quickly," when "he leans forward a little too eagerly," and when he expresses "an interest in their requests with a little too much solicitude"? It is simple: "he is playing at being a waiter in a café."

> This obligation is no different from what is expected of all merchants: their behavior is entirely ceremonial; people demand that they perform. There is the dance of the grocer, the tailor, the auctioneer, during which each one tries to persuade the customer that he is nothing more than a grocer, an auctioneer, a tailor.[8]

The list has no end: every social function is also a social fiction. Every temperament has its share of bad faith. You cannot be a doctor or a professor, whether marginal to the profession or just as you are supposed to be, nor can you be a great lawyer or writer, whether enthusiastic or blasé, without dancing the dance of your being: "When a man says, 'I am a difficult person,' he freely enters into a relationship with the state of being angry and at the same time interprets freely certain ambiguous details of his past."[9] The empire of representation has no limits: *Homo psychologicus* remains an actor. There is no true face hidden behind the masks and disguises that everyone puts on. You do not become perceptive by digging down deeply, discovering hidden secrets or mediocre motives below beautiful acts. People believe they get to know a man when they take him down a notch or two. In fact, this disillusion is itself deceiving, for it does not see the games and tricks of freedom behind the apparent consistency of nature. "To be a man," Sartre said, along with Gombrowicz, "means to pretend to be a man."[10] The least affected behavior is still playacting. People identified as being natural assume the pose needed to deserve being called natural. Once existence veers toward being an essence, it lies. Once man is, he makes believe. It does not follow, therefore, that life is only a stage even if "everywhere the role is there waiting for the right man."[11] In being conscious of being, man can never be what he is.

Hence the longing for coincidence, the aspiring for plenitude, the constant temptation to fill in the cracks; and, after the inevitable deceptions of the human comedy, the final resignation by some men of their humanity. Phenomenological description sustains moral judgment, leading Sartre to introduce unusual categories in his lecture on existentialism, substituting them for those traditionally used by the ruling language of philosophy: "Those who hide from total freedom, with solemnity or deterministic excuses, I call them cowards. As for those who try to show that their existence is necessary, when it is the very contingency of the appearance of man on earth, I call them bastards."[12]

If we return now to the anti-Semite, whose portrait Sartre made in the very same year that he wrote "Existentialism Is a Humanism," we see that the anti-Semite kills two birds with one stone. Having the qualities of both the coward and the bastard, the anti-Semite uses the idea of race to confer on his insubstantial humanity the thickness of nature and to persuade himself "that his place in the world has been marked out in advance, that it awaits him and that tradition has given him the right to occupy it."[13] Nothing contingent or intentional; he rests in the arms of being.

Emmanuel Lévinas was thinking about man's humanity at the same   **33**
time as Sartre, at the very moment humanity had disappeared. A less sensational philosopher than Sartre, he does not appear on Michel Foucault's list, yet he was more affected by the century than was the controversial French existentialist. Lévinas asked, "What is human?" This is the nagging question for a life and work dominated "by the foreboding and memory of the Nazi horror."[14]

The answer Lévinas proposed takes the form of a narrative. Disobeying Plato, who proclaimed that philosophy should not tell complicated tales, Lévinas discovered intrigue at the source of what makes us human. "Intrigue," moreover, guides his thought, which speaks of morality without creating a moral system. Ethics, according to Lévinas, is neither a sovereign good nor an immediate given that comes from knowing the difference between right or wrong. It is neither the law of God imposed on men from on high nor the manifestation in each man of his own autonomy: Ethics is first and foremost an event. Something must happen to me in order for me to stop being a "force that continues on its way" and wake up instead to pangs of conscience. This dramatic event is the encounter with the other, or more precisely, the revelation of the other's face.

An encounter, not a meeting; a revelation, not an unmasking. There is certainly a lot to read in a human face. This piece of skin is a mine of information because it always says more than its owner wishes. With a little training, we can learn to see a person's whole life in his face. But the face also has the strange power to take back what it confesses, to filter out the very signs that provide clues to the psychologist, sociologist, novelist, or Sherlock Holmes.

This is exactly the kind of power that Emilio Lussu came up against during his reconnaissance mission. He had gone out to learn something more, but in the end, what did he find facing him? "A man, A man! A man!" Repeating the same exclamation three times, he reveals the complete failure of Sherlock Holmes. Instead of accumulating more clues, the clues disappear. The interpretation fails to make the case; the argument has lost its grip. Of the person situated in a context, there remains in the end only pure abstraction.

But there is nothing dry about this abstraction. Nothing theoretical, intellectual, or cerebral. The face that abstracts itself from its own image is a bare face, that is to say, disarming, vulnerable, defenseless. Like the truth it hides, the face cannot be reduced to what it appears to be; it escapes even the uniform that identifies it. Stripped of all empirical properties, uprooted, without a country, it has nothing but its own helplessness to offer. "A face like mortality," to quote Lévinas again, "beyond the visibility of the phenomenon, beyond the abandonment of the victim."[15]

Abandonment and appeal: in the very anguish of the face, an incomparable force gives commands. Beyond the information contained in it, the face speaks in the imperative. Forsaken and exposed, it confesses nothing but orders instead, without theatrics, without puzzles requiring solutions, with only a thin silent voice that forbids killing. "The moral look measures the impenetrable infinity of the face where murderous intentions venture forth and then founder,"[16] wrote Lévinas, to which Lussu added, "A man! I could see the whites of his eyes, the features of his face. Dawn was rising, making it easier to see everything, and the sun was coming up from behind the mountains." Because he looks into his face, the face now concerns him, becomes his business. That man over there is no longer an object to do with as one wishes. He has become, without warning, a fellow man. Lussu is no longer spying on him; he is now watching out for him without even having consciously decided to do so. The tables have turned: Lussu finds himself serving, being ordered about, summoned by the very same person he was secretly observing and who was previously at his mercy. He was quietly making war when suddenly—"with the weakness of a being falling into humanity"[17]— the anxiety of peace swooped down on him and broke the charm.

The soldier Lussu plays no role in bringing about the changes that affect his actions. The interest he now takes in the Austrian officer does not flow from his own good intentions. On the contrary, his sense of what he should do is all shaken up. He is made uncomfortable by a disconcerting ultimatum, by an appeal coming from elsewhere, that is beyond his control.

Challenging Rousseau, who spoke of man's natural sweetness, and Tocqueville, who predicted that harsh feelings among men would melt away with equality, Lévinas described a painful and disturbing event. Where does this story of growing darkness come from? Answering his own question, Lévinas replied:

> The dramatic events of the 20th century and National Socialism, which overwhelmed a world built on the foundation of liberal principles. For better or worse, it was on this foundation of liberalism that the existence of the Jewish people rested and depended. Then came the events that tore from anti-Semitism its apocalyptic secret, revealing the extreme, demanding, and dangerous destiny of humankind.[18]

Kill anxieties about being; free life from all foreign interference; let it unfold without any hindrance; return to life its natural cruelty, its savage vitality, its spontaneity and arrogance; *silence individual faces* by reducing them to types or examples of a species; in the name of being social, substitute the brotherhood of races for the closeness one man feels for another. National Socialism's determination to eliminate the other demonstrates that the other possesses the ability to disturb the tranquillity of being.

How can a human catastrophe of such proportions take place at a time when man recognizes and understands how his fellow man feels? Because, if we follow Lévinas, this recognition does not inspire a burst of sentimental feeling but, rather, a sense of invasion. It does not appear as part of ourselves but as an inconvenience that upsets our plans, interrupts the flow of things, brutally weighing us down with a troublesome charge. An indirect consequence of a trauma like this is that it arouses a longing for a lost sense of wholeness, for an idyllic romance: "Nothing, in a sense, is more cumbersome than one's fellow man. Is not this desired one the undesirable itself?"[19] This is what Hitler's apocalypse has taught us. This all-out war, waged so that we could finally have peace, has instructed us, ironically, about a primary ethical fact and about the adventure of **36** Emilio Lussu.

In what we commonly call the postwar period, humanism became suddenly very old-fashioned. No longer compatible with the thinking of philosophers like Foucault, it soon gave way to structuralism. As Paul Ricoeur put it, structuralism is a "movement complex in its motivations, but one that had a single polemical vision" to relieve the thinking, speaking, acting subject of all his prerogatives.[20] The most private impulses, the most unpredictable moods, are attributed to inflexible systems. New experiences turn up unconscious processes or neutral and anonymous structures. The intention or genius of original works of inspiration is concealed from their creator and analyzed as games regulated by certain rules. Hardly visible at all to the author, said Roland Barthes, "these rules come from an age-old logic of narrative, from a symbolic form that constitutes us well before we are born, from that vast cultural space through which we personally . . . only pass through."[21]

The transformation here is spectacular. But why this fury against the subject? Why such exultation in making the subject fall from his throne? Why look for impersonal structures in the most intimate corners of an individual and his work, if not to bring the self back down to earth, to remind him of his humble origins—that he is only passing through—and to teach him that other selves are possible, people with other histories who are subjugated to other basic codes. The sense of horror in the face of Nazi racism turns into a rejection of colonialism—"the very humanistic, bourgeois Christian of the 20th century unconsciously harbors a Hitler within him,"[22] wrote Aimé Césaire in 1955—and the Sartrean bastard assumes the role of the self-important European.

All theoretical works identified with structuralism declare war on this sense of self-importance and infatuation with the subject. From postwar humanism to postcolonial antihumanism, the philosophical paradigm has been completely transformed, but the moral inspiration has remained the same. It is still a matter of shaking up the self-confident subject to the very core of his being, to make man anxious in order to make him more human.

It is because anxiety and inspiration went together under Communism that Stalin earned the title of humanist, a point Michel Foucault made sarcastically without developing it further. In the name of humanity, the Soviet Union and Western democracies joined forces and defeated Nazism. They fought, in other words, to beat back Hitler's attempt to erase the idea of fellow man from the face of the earth and to substitute in its place a vengeful natural hierarchy. What is more, in the eyes of the terrified humanist who emerged after the war, as in the eyes of his critic who embraced the struggle against colonialism, the country of revolution was philosophically superior to democracies: The Soviet Union conceded nothing to the idea of nature; it refused all half measures and pious declarations as responses to its demands.

For Marx, in effect, nothing is natural in either man or nature. Evil and suffering are socially constructed. They are not intrinsic to the human condition. Things are not things: they are social facts. As for that seemingly unalterable realm, supposedly not human, it is human in disguise. No countryside, no matter how bucolic, has meaning beyond its historical and social context: "The cherry-tree," Marx observed in a famous passage of *German Ideology*, "like almost all fruit-trees, was, as we know, transplanted by commerce into our zone only a few centuries ago. Thus, what Feuerbach sees as 'sensuous certainty' was merely the act of a specific society, at a specific time."[23] Beneath the sand, the cobblestones; beneath the appearance of what is given, the reality of conflict and of what has been constructed. What is more, the Marxists added, to pave the way for equality among men, everything produced by history must be passed over politically or destroyed.

Coming out of the war, the strength of Marxism resided in its radicalism and perfectionism. The beautiful words of liberalism could no more dull its clarity than control its will. When faced with the very real danger that collective identities might gain absolute power, declarations of universal humanity were not enough to combat it. As long as man sat on a throne in the heaven of ideas and a hierarchical system prevailed on earth, as long as a nominal or formal equality superimposed itself on real conditions of inequality, man was an impostor and a formidable one at that, for his role would continue to foster relationships of subordination even as he proclaimed, *urbi et orbi*, that he had put an end to them. Our humanism? "There you can see it quite naked and it is not a pretty sight," wrote Sartre in his famous and angry preface to Frantz Fanon's *The Wretched of the Earth*. "It was nothing but an ideology of lies, an exquisite justification for plundering. Its affectation and expressions of tenderness served as alibis for our acts of aggression. We established an abstract postulate of universality for the human race which served to cover up our real practices."[24] To keep the denunciation of the lords by humanists from obscuring social inequalities and the enslaved condition of colonized peoples, the abstract must immediately become concrete and humanity true to itself.

Those who belong to the working class will have to assume this task. They are different from other men, contemporary or historical. Members of the proletariat can in no way identify with determinations imposed on them by the period in which they live, by their social status or national affiliation. They live in the bourgeois period. Their nation is an artificial community for which they are asked to sacrifice their own interests in order to maintain the established order. As for their work, they have not had a job they can call their own for a very long time; work is an outside force. Banished from all conditions, even their own, excluded from all privileges, members of the proletariat have, in return, the ontological privilege of being nothing but human. Alienated from the world, they are protected from all the other possible forms of alienation from which men suffer when they take themselves for being who they are. If we follow Sartre and define the bastard as a man who believes that every place is his place because he has reserved a place for himself everywhere, then the proletarian is the antibastard par excellence. Unlike the bourgeois European or his imperialist variant, the self-important European, he does not need to stop history or turn man into an immovable essence to protect his interests. With him emerges the hope for a world delivered not only from bastards but also from the idea **39** of the bastard as a human possibility.

To prove the point, take the name given to his first country. As Jacques Derrida put it so well:

> The very name USSR is the only name of a state that makes no reference to a locality or nationality. The only proper noun of a state that has no given name in the usual sense of the term: The USSR is the name of the individual's state, the name of an individual and particular state that gave itself, or claimed to give itself, a name that has no reference to any one place or to any national past. From its very foundation, a state gave itself a name that was purely artificial, technical, conceptual, general, conventional, and constitutional, a "common" name, in sum, a communist name: a purely political name.[25]

In contrast to nationalistic countries, the USSR embodied this apotheosis: the country of humanity. A country all the same, since it certainly covered a vast territory—a sixth of the globe's surface and a tenth of its population, as its supporters liked to remind us—but a circumscribed territory. A country without roots, a nation without nature, a territory whose natives were not indigenous because, in this bastion of the new era, the institution won out over national origins, human intellect over the spirit of belonging to a certain place. With this victory, it was no longer valid to divide humanity into fellow countrymen and foreigners. Nobody can be a foreigner, no face challenged or left behind in the countryside. Nobody can be identified anymore in geographic terms but, rather, in technical terms. People can no longer be kept out: there is a place for everyone in a land bearing a common name.

Inclusive brotherhood of the common noun versus exclusive heredity of the proper noun: such was the humanistic charm of Stalin in 1945. As François Furet has argued, the movement against fascism em-

braced quite naturally the Communist idea and its supreme representative, and it did so not only because of the terrible battle of Stalin-
grad. Antifascists responded to a name that announced the end of an
existence surrounded by proprietary borders, a name that refused to
cut deals with local or historical determinations, to close men in and
divide up humanity.

Stalin's charm dulled rather quickly, but the humanism associated
with the name USSR continued for a long time to inspire political
struggle and intellectual work. It could be seen in general trends of
thought and in the theater of Brecht, leading Barthes to say in 1957
in an article entitled "Brecht, Marx and History," "To base his theater
on history [means] to refuse all essence to man, deny all reality to
human *nature* other than historical reality, to believe that there is no
eternal evil, only curable wrongs; it means to put the destiny of man
back in the hands of man himself."[26]

Following Marx, the personal enemy of thought became ideology
defined as "all those representations that make up the dominant class
in order to have it believe in the legitimacy and necessity of its own
domination, while hiding from it the very foundation of this domination."[27] In other words, in the name of ideology one fights against
rarely disguised illusions that present a particular point of view as a
universal truth. One fights as well against the illusion that hides the
progressive dimension of the world by bringing history to a halt, dis-
tracting slaves from their condition, thereby keeping them from
conceiving of the dangerous idea of throwing off the yoke.

As we see in the evolution of Michel Foucault's thought, this
antihumanist fury against the selfish claims of the subject will occupy only a brief moment in a broader project aimed at returning
to man the keys to his own destiny. In 1983 Foucault summarized
and recapitulated his work with the following formula: "Patient
labor giving form to our impatience for freedom."[28] His genealogical work is both meticulous and subversive. With documentary
support, he reveals the narrowness of our affective or mental universe. "What exists does not come close to filling up all the possible spaces."[29] That is the main teaching of an indiscreet and disre-

spectful discipline that uproots the most venerable customs or most sacred beliefs by digging up their origins, country by country. From this perspective, historical no longer means "respectable" but, rather, "revocable," and the archivist-philosopher sentences to **41** death the codes of conduct he has uncovered. "My role," Foucault explained, "and that is too strong a word, is to show people that they are freer than they think, that they take as true, or obvious, certain themes that have been produced at a particular moment in history and that this so-called evidence can be criticized and destroyed."[30] Historical investigation thus delivers people from the idea of nature to emancipate them more fully from their history. As malicious as it is detailed, Foucault's erudition discovers the "immense and growing number of ways to criticize things."[31] Instead of focusing on transcending what makes us dependent, he notes the "fragility . . . in the very bedrock of existence,"[32] which was once considered to be solid and familiar. By analyzing the limits imposed on us, Foucault continued, we can show how penetrable these limits are. And with his critique, this paradoxical positivist wants to destroy the power of positivities: "To free the possibility of not being, doing, or thinking from the contingencies of life that have made us what we are, think, or do." [33]

By assigning this task to current work in philosophical criticism, Foucault—in a way different from Sartre but certainly like Sartre—is rebelling against "everything in the human being that we can indicate with the words: *this is*."[34] When he denounces humanist thought that prescribes a model for man, that attributes an essence to him or weighs him down with a definition, he is struggling against the same enemy as his enemy. When he says that man does not have to go out and discover his own being but must invent himself, develop himself, or manufacture himself, he is going a little less far than Sartre but is still renewing ties to the first humanism: the one that came out of the Middle Ages and celebrated in man "a creation, of an undefined type" on whom falls the burden and perilous honor of fashioning his being, of shaping it and giving it form through virtue and art.

Feverishly reconstituted, the humanism of Pico della Mirandola lives on after a war in which the losing side threatened that humanity would disappear into nature. Returning once again in the guise of postmodern morality and thought, we see that this morality is not moralizing and this humanism is not soft. But can one remain committed to this kind of morality and thought and draw any lesson from the twentieth century? Can this new form of humanism explain how individuals espousing the most radical will to free humanity from its chains could produce a world of concentration camps like the ones produced by those who submitted themselves to the most rigid form of determinism?

three

The Triumph of the Will

IN 1927, JULIEN BENDA published *The Treason of the Intellectuals*. The book came out more than thirty years after the beginning of the Dreyfus affair. An active supporter of the framed Jewish colonel, Benda had never forgotten what happened in France at the turn of the century. With the past firmly in mind, the celebrated essayist accused intellectuals of betraying the values they were expected to honor when they abandoned a disinterested universalism in favor of emotionally charged particularisms. Instead of protecting their minions, intellectuals defended national values and "ethnic inflections," making people ashamed "of aspiring to what is general and transcendent in all men."[1] They also called on members of the working class to drop "justice in itself," "humanity in itself,"[2] and the other prominent features of idealism.

Race or class, proclaimed Benda, is one and the same thing. Try as they might to be different, the passions of reaction and the passions of revolution resemble each other. While fighting, supposedly on opposite sides, they deliver the same moral and universal truth: both camps have contempt for individual men. Rejecting the cult of the self, they support instead an idolatrous allegiance to the group, and they do so without shame. As Benda saw it, ideologues representing both the right and the left are motivated by the same sense of sacred selfishness. On one side, this selfishness leads to drunken excesses, even barbarism, in the name of the nation; on the other, to inspiring the proletariat "to sink down into the consciousness of their *special* interest, create for themselves a *special* sense of morality, a *special* kind of intelligence, abolish in their hearts the idea that there exists an essential community between them and members of the other class."[3]

Benda owes his place in posterity to *The Treason of the Intellectuals*. Of his many works, only this one remains famous. Not a year goes by, not even part of a year, not even a week, without somebody paying tribute to his book in an impassioned editorial against intellectual abjuration. Benda, however, lost his way. He had an intuition, made the right comparison, but based his critique on the wrong analysis. Locked into dialectical thinking, he did not grasp the relationship in Communism between the particular and the universal. Had he grasped it, he would have seen that if Communism calls on the proletariat to break its bonds of solidarity with men from the other class, it is only to build a new society on the corpse of bourgeois society and finally to achieve universal solidarity. If the interest of the working-class man is sacred, it is because, in contrast to his enemies, he carries the promise into history of emancipation for all. And if the workers' party is called the Party, with a capital P, it is because it is not simply a party but the totality: the idea of the proletariat is big enough to embrace the entire human species. Louis Althusser drove the point home in a talk he gave on February 2, 1968, to the French Philosophical Society, when he described Lenin as having "a wholehearted, open laugh that the fishermen of Capri recognized as belonging to one of their kind, to somebody on their side."[4]

Benda himself saw the light twenty years later and did not have to die in ignorance. In 1949 the universalism of Communism was revealed to him when the Hungarian minister Rajk stood trial for joining forces with Tito's Yugoslavia in an anti-Soviet plot. Concurring with the judges who found Rajk guilty, Benda noted:

> At the time of the Dreyfus affair, the partisans of order concluded that Esterhazy's confession was not proof. The Hungarian

enemies of justice and their international allies have done even better. They maintain that the confessions of Rajk and his accomplices demonstrate that they have not committed the acts of which they are accused.[5]

Did Benda have to repudiate his principles in order to be duped by a trumped-up trial? Not exactly. The explanation for the change is simple: the war. And for this uncompromising metaphysician, the war in question is the life-and-death struggle between the two adversaries he identifies in *The Treason of the Intellectuals*: the Enlightenment and Romanticism. This is the war of the universal against the particular, fought to protect the human spirit from taking root in the soil of the fatherland; to keep the mind free from tradition, action from custom, thought from language. Benda was, or believed he was, on familiar ground, until Nazism turned Bolshevism into the absolute enemy. From that moment on, it became impossible to see the revolution as romanticism on the left, a working-class variation on a reactionary theme. Hitler had just given Communism its universalistic dimension, and, in doing so, allowed it to take its place in the avant-garde of the Enlightenment. Hence the tentative endorsement by the last living Dreyfusard of the trial and verdict against Rajk.

Hence also the resistance of intellectuals in Europe for many years to Hannah Arendt's *Origins of Totalitarianism*, which was published in 1951. How can the same term describe two systems, so diametrically opposed, whose antagonism for each other had just been sealed by the blood of millions of people? The only thing total, or totalizing, here is the war that made Nazism and Bolshevism enemies. But six years after the Reich had fallen, the similarities between the two systems were glaring. They stared you in the face.

Hannah Arendt did not deliberately choose to put herself in this delicate, even risky, position. Contrary to what some may have thought, she was not motivated by a cold-war mentality or by wanting to demonize the enemy of her adopted homeland. Having no accounts to settle with Communism, she set out to answer the following questions: "*What happened? Why did it happen? How could it have happened*"?[6] It was Hitler's apocalypse that motivated her. When she began her research in 1943, she described the book as "a project to try to think about the *uselessness* of the massacre of the Jews."[7] The sacrilegious analogy insinuated itself gradually in 1947 with the discovery of the Soviet camps; it then developed philosophically from a truly original understanding of the Nazi terror.

Hannah Arendt agreed with her contemporaries that the doctrine of National Socialism crushed human freedom under the weight of ethnic determinations. But this alone did not describe its underlying evil. Nazi racism, she continued, is based on a reading of nature that divides the human species into distinct humanities. In a fantastically rigorous way, it rejects the idea of a universal morality while offering a universal system of explanation. For National Socialists, all roads lead to the Jew. Not only is the Jew different; he is evil, invisible, and omnipotent. The very fact of his dispersion is proof of his desire to subjugate people everywhere and make off with everything.

Discovering *The Protocols of the Elders of Zion* in 1920, Hitler gratefully acknowledged that this document revealed "with truly horrifying reliability, the nature and activity of the Jewish people, by exposing 'their inner logic and their final aims.'"[8] Passionate in his hatred, the force of Hitler's feelings as expressed in these lines was less remarkable for its virulence than for its claim to explain history. Hitler's hatred did not stop with merely hating. Intensity was not the determining factor. What characterized the hatred was its power to see and divulge. This kind of anti-Semitism is never caught by surprise; it substitutes the transparent opacity of the plot for the anarchy of the visible world. Crazy, yes, but in Chesterton's sense of the term: It is not the Nazi who has lost his mind. It is man who, having lost everything but reason, challenges the facts, always throwing up obstacles, for the benefit of a coherence that cannot be proved false. Was *The Protocols of the Elders of Zion* invented to serve the propaganda machine of the czar's police? It was not for nothing, Hitler responded, "that the *Frankfurter Zeitung* is forever moaning to the public that it [*The Protocols*] is supposed to be based on a forgery"; this "is the surest proof that it is genuine." The Jews are conspiring; now their conspiracy has been discovered. They must therefore have us believe that *The Protocols* is a fable and call it mystification.

In destroying common sense, not reason, as Lukács diagnosed it, **47** by means of a logic entirely self-referential, this quibbling and inexorable racism broke decisively with reactionary thinking and abandoned the heritage of the Counterrevolution. In the historical period that dates from 1789 to 1793—that is, from the Declaration of the Rights of Man to the Jacobin dictatorship—spokesmen for the Counterrevolution dramatically showed how "man, acting by himself and without religion, is unable to break any chains that oppress him without sinking in the process still deeper into slavery."[9] The overthrow of radical liberation by unlimited terror is the punishment that man suffers for his sacrilegious putsch, for wanting to take the place of God and become both the actor in and the author of his own history. Man has forgotten the Fall, warned the great reactionaries in thunderous voices. That is why he has fallen so low and hurt himself so badly.

The anti-Semitism of the Nazis says nothing of the kind. It makes no reference to the corruption of human nature; instead, it denounces tirelessly the conspiracy of the Evil Ones. The solemn accusation against the audacity of Prometheus gives way to a merciless battle against the enemy of the human race. Original sin is no longer invoked to subdue the will of man, to convince him of the foolishness of change and bring him back to reason, that is, to obedience. Now it is reason that, free of all constraints, shows man that a clandestine power is at the source of all that disgraces and bothers him. This logic, held back by nothing, is gratifying in that it eliminates with a single statement random events and personal responsibility, the role of chance and human error.

In the Nazi vision of the world, there is no place for whims of fortune or the revenge of heaven. The misfortune that afflicts me never occurs by chance or by my own deficiencies but by acts of the invisible, a villain with tentacles whose perversity I suffer daily. Sin is no longer in me but—formidable transference—in him. I am not fallible,

I am martyred. To the objections raised against divine justice, Joseph de Maistre responded—"No man is ever punished for being just, but for being a man. It is therefore false to say that virtue suffers in this world; it is human nature that suffers and it always deserves to."[10] In the world in which the Nazis live, which has no divine power, evil is no longer "a transcendent question concerning, so to speak, political matters outside humanity" but "an immanent question concerning internal politics."[11] Suffering, formerly accepted as expiation, now becomes a form of aggression. Paranoia steps out in front of neurosis. Taking the place of the counterrevolutionary explanation, which was austere and self-reproachful—"you are a victim, because you are guilty"—comes the revolutionary and terrifying "you are a victim because of the Jews."

"Don't you think that you are attributing rather too much importance to the Jews?" Rauschning timidly asked the chancellor of the Reich when he had his ear. "No! No! No!" exclaimed Hitler. "It is impossible to exaggerate the formidable quality of the Jew as an enemy."[12] The great Céline said the same thing in his inimitable fashion, "The Aryans are always cuckolded."

We are thousands of miles away from Edmund Burke's "Massacre, torture, hanging! These are your rights of men!"[13] Warnings against immoderate behavior have given way to the extravagant idea that everything is possible. After recognizing the strength, subtlety, and ubiquity of the enemy, Hitler logically concluded that it was time to act: "There is no point trying to negotiate with the Jew, only to decide: all or nothing! As for me, I have decided to take political action."[14]

All or nothing: Hitler introduced this radical principle into politics because in his universe, nothing could escape the logic of war, absolutely nothing. Even nature lacked the reassuring stability of nature. As Hannah Arendt explained it:

> Underlying the Nazis' belief in race . . . is Darwin's idea of man as the product of a natural development which does not necessarily stop with the present species of human beings. . . .

Darwin's introduction of the concept of development into nature, his insistence that, at least in the field of biology, natural movement is not circular but unilinear, moving in an infinitely progressing direction, means in fact that nature is, as it were, being swept into history, that natural life is considered to be historical.[15]

Nietzsche got it right: the twentieth century has staged a war for the domination of the world in the name of philosophical principles. But contrary to the way it is usually interpreted, it has not been a war of a historical vision of humanity against a natural one. It is true that Nazism may define man as a natural being, blithely subordinating the mind to natural life, but the life it exalts is not a life without history. It values iron and production, not stones and motionlessness. Whereas reactionary thought identifies change with evil, for Hitler, change is good. Nature keeps moving and advancing; it never stops developing. To interpret the laws of this movement and reach a verdict: that is the mission of the Führer. If he fiercely attacks democracy, it is because this political system stands in the way of evolution. In protecting the weak, it interferes with the development of the species. If he wants the Jews dead, it is to free humanity and lead it to achieve its final goal. Convinced though he might have been of the inequality of the races, Hitler was no more the heir of Gobineau than he was of Joseph de Maistre, Edmund Burke, or Adam Müller.

Gobineau was actually a melancholy thinker, something that Tocqueville recognized. Writing to his dear friend and adversary after the publication of Gobineau's *Essay on the Inequality of the Human Races*, Tocqueville said:

> I never concealed from you that I am greatly prejudiced against what seems to be your main idea which, I must confess, seems to belong to a group of materialistic theories. Moreover, it is one of its most dangerous members, for it applies fatalism not merely to individuals but to those perennial conglomerations of individuals called races.[16]

The century was fifty-three years old, and the book, according to Tocqueville, came out when the tide had already turned, arriving in a Europe exhausted by self-determinism:

> In the last century we were too confident, in an exaggerated and somewhat childish way, in the power that man held over himself and that peoples had over their destinies. That was the error of those times. . . . Now we live in a period of excesses in the opposite direction. Today we believe that we can do nothing and like to think that struggle and effort are henceforth useless, that our blood, muscles and nerves will always be stronger than our will and virtue. Strictly speaking, this is the great sickness of our time, the very opposite of the sickness of our fathers.[17]

Hitler's racism, on the other hand, had no trace of this languor and weariness, no symptom of the sickness. For the Führer, there was no point even in debating the possibility of improving humanity. His idea of race did not reveal the force of determinism—the permanence of racial traits or their fatal degradation—but the characteristics of the enemy and the cosmic dimension of combat needed to oppose it. The struggle for life identifies the political arena as the place for deciding the future of the human species. Any frustration or hindrance to an act should be dismissed with a single gesture. There are no objective limits to what is doable, only subjective levels of resistance that can be eliminated. Any obstacle standing in the way of a scheme, any interference between a desired goal and its execution, must be the work of a saboteur. If things do not work out exactly as planned, this is not due to the existence of others but to the malevolence of the Other. Adversity always comes from the adversary. Public space is a battlefield. Thus in order to win the battle, it is necessary to get on the same wavelength with the adversary, to make oneself as universal as he. "The conception of the nation has become meaningless," Hitler confided to Rauschning.

> The conditions of the time compelled me to begin on the basis of that conception. But I realized from the first that it could

have only transient validity. The "nation" is a political expedient of democracy and Liberalism. We have to get rid of this false conception and set in its place the conception of race, which has not yet been politically used up. The new order cannot be conceived in terms of the national boundaries of peoples with an historical past, but in terms of race that transcends those boundaries. All the adjustments and corrections of frontiers and regions of colonization, are like plowing on sand. . . . Do you understand what I mean? I have to liberate the world from dependence on its historical past. Nations are the outward and visible forms of our history. So I have to fuse these nations into a higher order if I want to get rid of the chaos of an historic past that has become an absurdity. . . . With the concept of race, National Socialism will carry its revolution abroad and recast the world.[18]

National politics *participated* in human history, whereas racial politics *constructs* the history of humanity. No longer the theater of multiple and intersecting adventures, history becomes a single manufactured process and part of an architectural plan. It is no longer a matter of *doing* it with but of *making* or creating. Radicalizing the power of making in this way leads to idealizing cruelty and turning evil into a puritanical ethic. Nazis must commit violence not out of a taste for it but out of duty, not out of sadism but out of virtue, not out of pleasure but as part of a method, not out of savage impulses but in the name of higher principles. The tools of Nazi violence must be placed in the hands of those endowed with the competence of a professional and with the persistent concern that the job must get done. As Hannah Arendt put it:

Just as the law in civilized countries assumes that the voice of conscience tells everybody "Thou shalt not kill," even though man's natural desires and inclinations may at times be murderous, so the law of Hitler's land demanded that the voice of conscience tell everybody: "Thou shalt kill," although the organizers of the massacres knew full well that murder is against the normal desires and inclinations of most people. Evil in the Third Reich had lost the quality by which most people recognize it—the quality of temptation.[19]

In other words, Hitler did not institute a reign of crime on the ruins of a moral order but gave crime all the appearance—and apparatus—of a moral order, with obligations and sanctions. "Because laws are generally harsh," Péguy used to say, "we believe that everything that is harsh is necessarily law."[20] Because virtue is difficult, we believe that what is difficult is virtuous: the SS state used this misunderstanding to justify struggling against compassion in the name of resisting temptation and against the inclination to give in to weakness before the imperious misery of a human face. National Socialism fought the Ten Commandments by forgery, not debauchery; it chose to climb the steep slope of asceticism to free man from the anxieties of being and from the pressures of having the old man within him: "When they get going, rigidly immoral people are far more dangerous than flexible ones. For in being rigid, they are easily accepted as representing the law."[21]

Coming to "the most difficult question" about the fate of the Jews, Heinrich Himmler exhorted his inner circle of SS officers to be strong, that is, to be deaf to the innumerable petitions that say, "Of course all Jews are swine, except this one and that one, who are good Jews and against whom nothing should be done."[22] To have pity was dangerous in the eyes of the Reichsführer SS because it allowed for exceptions. And when you make an exception, you are no longer doing but once again doing with; siding with the enemy at the very moment when the bells are ringing to annihilate him; coming to terms with the reality of the world instead of resolutely fashioning it the way you want it to be; falling from what is absolute into what is relative; betraying the radical demands of history for a traditional solution with diplomatic accommodation and compromise.

Himmler, moreover, saw venality and tenderness as the same thing. Greed and charity, letting oneself be corrupted or being swayed by sympathy—two reprehensible temptations, two acts unfaithful to history, two aberrations of sensibility, two ways out that are equally wrong. Thus, he noted in the same speech, "We have no right to take a single *pfennig* off property confiscated from Jews. Since the very beginning I have decreed that any SS man who took even a *mark* would be condemned to death."[23] The majesty of duty, as the other one used to say, has nothing to do with the pleasures of life.

As we have already noted, Hannah Arendt decided to look at totalitarianism out of a sense of amazement before the utter uselessness of the extermination. How could the Nazis, she wondered, and we continue to wonder, do something so clearly against their interest and methodically massacre a large and free workforce, one that was qualified and available forever? Anticipating the question, the head of the Gestapo replied that no utilitarian or material consideration, no economic or strategic calculation, should push back the date or stain the purity of this operation, carried out for the salvation of Germany and humankind. "If Germany frees itself from the Jewish stranglehold," Hitler wrote in *Mein Kampf* when he was still only an insignificant troublemaker, "we will be able to say that the greatest danger facing people everywhere has been destroyed for the entire universe."[24] And when the time came to carry out this immense project, it would be necessary to know how to assume the responsibility. "I think you know me well enough, gentlemen," Himmler declared to his generals on May 24, 1944,

> to recognize that I am not bloodthirsty and that I get no pleasure out of doing what is difficult and painful. But I can also lay claim to this: I have a strong enough nervous system and a sense of duty sufficiently well developed for me to carry out something I recognize as a necessity.[25]

This necessity, for which Himmler sacrificed both his interests and inclinations, is evolution, a process that does not stop with the human species as it presently is but continues moving forward without weakness until the very end.

In contrast to Sartre's anti-Semite, the Nazi criminal does not need the enemy in order to feel naturally superior or to see himself, without doing a thing, as a member of an elite and a subject with rights. He does not flee his uncomfortable freedom by hating a pernicious and inferior being; instead, he projects onto this being his own negation of all boundaries. Drawing the line between "them and us" for everyone on the planet, he does not refuse to accept his condition as a free man but, rather, the inherent limits imposed on the human condition.

This racism, like all other forms of racism, certainly accepts—even demands—a kind of determinism. The claims of individual consciousness are denounced in the name of hereditary constraints and the laws of the collective unconscious. In exchange for the paradoxical privilege that humanism confers on man—from Pico della Mirandola to Sartre—of being in the beginning absolutely nothing, Hitler's doctrine offered the final imprisonment of beings in their being. But instead of humiliating the will, in the way that reactionary thought or classical racism does, this fanaticism of assignation joins forces with the fanaticism of action and proclaims the triumph of the will over all forms of finitude.

The triumph of the will over all forms of finitude is also the formula of Stalinist Communism. There are, of course, many differences between the state envisioned by the SS and the regime created by the Soviets. These have to do with the nature of authority, economic conditions, and the social makeup of the party and also with the values put forward, objectives pursued, and the scale and duties of terror. As historian Ian Kershaw quite rightly noted, "Even if we admit that the reign of Stalinist terror was popular among members of different parts of the population, the low level of popularity leaves one to assume that the regime could not depend on having the same wide consensus that Hitler's regime had."[26] There remains, however, the same ontological core: in the two systems, social phenomena are understood as processes and forms, as forces in movement. For each one, we can say, repeating Chesterton's formula to explain evolution, "There is no such thing as a thing. At best there is only one thing, and that is a flux of everything and anything."[27] Here and there, certainty swims willingly with the current. Class warfare, racial warfare—despite the differences in values—we see the same "everything is possible" unfold over the battlefield, the same political conception of omnipotence, the same breathtaking absence of scruples toward facts, the same philosophical and paranoid conviction that nothing exists independent of a conflict of wills. In both systems, radicality more than savagery stimulates crime, justifying the logic of their positions, and leading them to accept the final consequences, without hesitation or prevarication.

In Arthur Koestler's *Darkness at Noon*, the hero, Rubashov, is a member of the Bolshevik old guard who had participated in the October Revolution. Thrown into prison by Stalin (known in the novel as "Number 1," a name that is no longer a name), he rebels against his fate. In his cell he thinks about how the revolution became bankrupt, got stuck in the mud. Then he grows tired or, rather, begins to lose the physical, moral, and intellectual strength necessary to protect himself against a line of reasoning that turns him into the kind of victim that he had vindictively turned others into in the past. Rubashov signs the confession he is asked to sign and pleads guilty at the trial. Guilty of what? Of "having followed sentimental impulses, and in so doing [of having] been led into contradiction with historical necessity." Clarifying the point further before his magistrate instructor, Rubashov adds:

> I have lent my ear to the laments of the sacrificed and thus became deaf to the arguments which proved the necessity to sacrifice them. I plead guilty to having rated the question of guilt and innocence higher than that of utility and harmfulness. *Finally, I plead guilty to having placed the idea of man above the idea of mankind.*[28]

After being worn down, Rubashov finally capitulates and falls into the trap, accepting in the end the arguments of the judge, who, like Rubashov himself, belongs to the generation of the founding fathers. To give in to your conscience, his comrade Ivanov tells him, is to fail in your duty to humanity.

There are only two conceptions of human ethics, and they are at opposite poles. One of them, Christian and humane, declares the individual to be sacrosanct, and asserts that the rules of arithmetic are not to be applied to human units. The other starts from the basic principle that a collective aim justifies all means, and not only allows, but demands, that the individual should in every way be subordinated and sacrificed to the community—which may dispose of him as a laboratory rabbit or a sacrificial lamb. The first conception could be called antivivisection morality; the second, vivisection morality. . . . Have you ever read brochures of an antivivisectionist society? They are shattering and heartbreaking; when one reads how some poor mutt which has had its liver cut out whines and licks his tormentor's hands, one is just as nauseated as you were tonight. But if these people had their say, we would have no serums against cholera, typhoid or diphtheria.[29]

The analogy between animal experiments and human sacrifices is not, to put it mildly, immediately obvious. But before denouncing the analogy as sophism or scandal, let us think for a minute about what it means. Ivanov wants to analyze the conflict between pity and reason. Reason maintains and illustrates the existence of a separate human kingdom. Pity denies this claim to the extent that—as Rousseau clearly saw—it is repulsed not only by seeing man suffer but also by seeing man as a completely suffering being. In the name of reason, man assumes the right to split humanity off from animality; but with pity, man crosses the line once again and identifies with the poor little moaning dog, with these miserable living laboratories, what little we see of them—these product-making machines and their intensive breeding operations that have turned animals into consumer products. Thus the same word, *humanity*, identifies simultaneously a kingdom apart and provides the argument for opposing the separation—a distinct species and a sensibility that defies making the distinction.

What happens, then, when equality increases and forced identifications are rejected, whether, to paraphrase Lévi-Strauss, it is a matter of an entire culture rejecting its own cultural identification or an individual member of a culture rejecting the role or social function his culture tried to impose on him?[30] What happens is that the culture or individual claims the right to choose its own or his own identification, which, as Lévi-Strauss showed, interpreting Rousseau, "can only realize itself *beyond man* with all that is alive and, consequently suffers; an identification also *before* the function or character, with a being not yet formed, but given."[31] In other words, man goes beyond his limits: he no longer contains himself; *his heart does not know which way to turn.* It matters little whether he confronts foreigners, enemies, or animals; they all are beasts deprived of language and reason. Vulnerability and fear endow them all with their own identity.

With this empathy there is not the slightest hint of vitalism. Led off the beaten path by pity, man does not discover his animal side at the end of the road. He would never dream of taking a stand in the name of instinctual drives that inhibit and deaden the reign of the spirit. Nor would he declare the struggle for life to be the only law of being. It is not the spectacle of life that gives birth to his feelings but the threat of death, not the wild animal but the catch, not the voluptuous annihilation of man in nature but the extension of the community of mortals to other creatures and not only to members of the human species.

Pity is therefore not fascist but, as Ivanov would say, foolish, and for two reasons: foolish because it forgets, for the benefit of poor creatures, the needs of men, and foolish more generally because it does not know how to raise the particular case of misery that man sees before his eyes to the level of a universal project. For Ivanov the defenders of animals prove that man has lost his way because he has human feelings. Both reason and justice demand that man get hold of himself. Superior to pity, justice cares too much about the fate of the human community to allow itself to fall into the trap of pity when confronted with a crying face or the anguish of a particular individual.

Of course, we cannot sit back passively and accept the totalitarian argument for rejecting pity and defending a system that crushes men by likening it to modernity's argument for killing animals: a necessary evil to improve society's ability to feed, dress, and care for its people. But perhaps it is not entirely unreasonable to open up a new debate

58 of Valladolid and invite Ivanov to participate. In his speciously woven argument, Ivanov may have revealed a hidden truth, applied for the good of a bad cause, which can be summarized as follows:

> People can only express qualities associated with true human goodness when faced with beings that have no power. Mankind's true moral test, the fundamental test (which lies deeply buried from view) is the way he treats those who are entirely at his mercy: animals. In taking this test, man has failed miserably, and his failure has led to a disaster so basic that it has affected all other disasters.[32]

In the end, Koestler's logician-judge compromises the very idea of humanity in the way he praises and practices inhuman acts. In contrast to followers of Nazi doctrine, he is obsessed by justice, not power. He does not fight to establish a racial hierarchy but to create an authentically egalitarian and homogeneous society; he does not want to free the strong and eliminate morality; he wants to avenge the weak, for he takes morality seriously. Despite all the differences, Ivanov calls Doktor Pannwitz to mind, for they both share the conviction that history has overwhelmed compassion. This history has set the stage for humanity to sacrifice basic, self-evident human ties in the name of progress.

Rather than speak about regression the way Lévi-Strauss does, we must recognize instead that the twentieth century has pitted dignity against history. This battle of two aspects of the modern idea of humanity has ended in the bloody triumph of history over dignity, of mankind over individual human beings. By virtue of his humanity, the concept of dignity gives each individual an intrinsic and absolute value: "Man's dignity demands that he be seen . . . in his particularity and, as such, be seen . . . as reflecting mankind in general."[33] In contrast, the concept of history or of human progress sees the value of individual human beings in relative terms, proclaiming the ontological supremacy of the life of humanity over the life of men. "The principle: there are only individuals, is true as a physical fact and not as a teleological proposition,"[34] wrote Renan in *L'Avenir de la science* (The future of science), this bible of progress. "In the overall plan, the individual disappears." Continuing in the same vein, Renan asked:

> What is this man doing to me, putting himself between me and humanity? . . . True nobility does not mean having a name of one's own or individual genius but belonging to the noble race of the sons of God, to be a soldier lost in the immense army advancing to conquer the perfect.[35]

In a crowning gesture to the century and thought of the Enlightenment, Kant affirmed together, and with equal weight, the dignity of all men and the progress of humanity. Having ourselves been educated in a century that embraced the grandiose images of *L'Avenir de la science*, we speak more cautiously than Kant and claim with Hannah Arendt: "It is against human dignity to believe in progress."[36] All the more so, we might add, when expectations are great. For if progress leads to the conquest and realization of the perfect, that is, to helping man achieve reaching absolute sovereignty; if the mission of history makes it possible to free humanity from finitude by giving man the divine attributes of omniscience and omnipotence, then the servants of history must account for the way history marks time and has delays, reversals, and moments of backsliding. They can no longer dismiss misfortune as heavenly justice or the deceitfulness of the devil. They need an entirely new explanation.

The time has come, in other words, for the servants of history to prove that the enemy is the cause of our misfortunes. God is dead; everybody is an enemy. Our failures reveal the enemy's evil acts, not our finitude. Even our finitude is his fault, not our fate. We must therefore destroy the enemy in order to achieve history's great promise. Comrade Rubashov is killed only after having been convinced that he has committed acts of sabotage for counterrevolutionary causes in the service of a foreign power.

In proving the enemy wrong, totalitarian thought achieves its goal of not perceiving reality as it is and not seeing events as they come along. It bases its proof on the "indisputable certainty" that man must fight until death the enemy of the human species. With this certainty, totalitarian thought frees itself "from the reality that we perceive with our five senses and insists on a 'truer' reality concealed behind all perceptible things, dominating them from this place of concealment and requiring a sixth sense that enables us to become aware of it."[37]

Hannah Arendt gave the name *ideology* to this sixth sense and to this way of thinking, which is emancipated from all experience by its power to explain everything. With ideology, be it racist or communist, "the concept of enmity is replaced by that of conspiracy, and this produces a mentality in which reality—real enmity or real friendship—is no longer experienced or understood in its own terms, but is automatically assumed to signify something else."[38] Challenging the logic of ideological thinking, Hannah Arendt takes the opposite point of view from Marx and from those who, after the war and because of the war, laid claim to the Marxist concept of ideology and did away with the idea of nature. For Arendt, ideology is not the lie of appearances; rather, it is the suspicion cast on appearances and on the systematic presentation of reality as being a superficial and deceptive screen. It is not perceptive faith but incredulity. It is not the naive acceptance of what is visible but the knowledgeable dismissal of it. In a word, it is not the fraudulent erasure of history under the timelessness of essence but the reabsorption of the uncontrollable "there is" into the indetermination of the world, the reabsorption of the troubling diversity of events into a historical drama with two characters, both of whom have been shielded from sight and given to knowledge.

"Everything is described with efficiency when facts leave the order of a false Nature and reinstate themselves into the true order of History," asserted Roland Barthes in an article entitled "Humanism Without Words," which appeared in 1951, in the same year as *The Origins of Totalitarianism*. "It is because nothing in the past exists outside historical reason that the future can become entirely the property of the men who make it."[39]

For Barthes, ideology or mystification is the recognition of an irreducible excess of being in thought, the affirmation of the noncoincidence of the real and the rational and the renunciation by humanity of having complete control over its destiny. For Arendt, on the contrary, ideology is the negation of the uncertain, the refusal to accept the unpredictable in human affairs and in those forms of interaction in which one relinquishes something: an event, an encounter, a moment already there. In other words, Arendt saw ideology as erasing all boundaries and suppressing the very idea of adventure by the concept of history.

Ideology: one word, two meanings. This is not an unfortunate homonym but a major difference of opinion: in decreeing that only ideological barriers stand in the way of achieving a sovereign humanity, we go back to the kind of thinking that led to the evil of this century. We can reflect on this evil only by revealing the murderous denial of finitude at the heart of the idea that man can do everything.

four

The Irony of History

THE IDEA OF PROGRESS was thriving at the end of the nineteenth century. Developed in works on the philosophy of history, it celebrates the endless perfectibility of man, who forever makes conquests and advances in science. Appearing first at the dawn of modern times, this idea has turned the philosophical tradition around: violence, which defied *logos* from time immemorial, has changed signs and become a positive force. Evil is now good and violence useful, for they serve higher ends, bringing humanity closer to fulfilling itself. Sharing this same view of progress are those who espouse Hegel's dialectic, or trick of reason, Marx's class struggle, and Darwin's law of evolution.

"In the nineteenth century History replaces God as the all powerful force in the destiny of men," wrote François Furet, "but only in the twentieth century do we see the political madness caused by this substitution."[1] What people dreamed about doing in the previous century became possible and occurred in our own, right under our eyes, obscuring the significance of the achievement. Before making the transition from one age to the other, we turned progress into the god of reality and made sure that history would continue to reign. In doing so, we overlooked the great irony of our time, the literally unbearable paradox of the twentieth century: believing in history and the irresistible achievement of humanity while watching two radically antagonistic versions of history produce similar regimes. If we face this twentieth-century paradox today, it is thanks to a prior event for which we have never found a satisfactory explanation: World War I.

64   This war certainly had causes. It did not break out like an unexpected clap of thunder in a cloudless sky, in a Europe peacefully governed by a balance of powers. It caught nobody by surprise; every country had been arming itself for years. "There is the kind of warrior society in which everyone thinks about the beauty of combat and the kind in which everyone thinks about proclaiming victory," wrote Péguy on the eve of the Great War. "One thinks about chivalry and the other about empire." One is a system based on the rules of honor; the other on domination. There is Achilles, the man who exposes himself and fights, and Ulysses, "the man who keeps quiet and wins."[2]

For Péguy, of course, Achilles was French and Ulysses German. But let us be fair: since 1911 and the second conflict over Morocco, every European power had statesmen ready to draw their swords to thwart the expansionist designs of rival states. As Stefan Zweig reminded us in *The World of Yesterday*, aspiring heroes in every state dreamed of taking an illegal and dangerous trip to some far-off romantic place to escape the restrictions imposed on them by the bourgeois universe of laws and documents, by what had already become the machine-driven, mechanistic world of work. Back in Europe, the Continent was tormented by so many dreams, fears, and reasoned explanations that no one thought seriously about trying to stop the machine once the switch was turned on at Sarajevo on June 28, 1914. In contrast to the armed conflicts taking place in the days of Bismarck, the main adversaries here did not start this strange war. Still, the machines on both sides went automatically into gear, for everyone anticipated the hostilities and knew the war was about to begin.

No sooner had war been declared than the process took on a life of its own that neither reason nor dream could control. Between anticipating its outbreak and the actual event, there was what Raymond Aron called the *shock of technology*. Government leaders and their advisers confidently assumed that they were engaged in a war like any other. They would, they believed, win a decisive victory in a matter of a few weeks. Instead, all their lightning attacks failed: Austria's offensive against Serbia, Russia's against Austria in Galicia and against Germany in East Prussia, France's attack on Germany in the Lorraine and Ardennes, and finally the German offensive against Belgium and France. The military power of the armies far exceeded all expectations. Necessity demanded a war economy, strategies of attrition, and graves in the trenches: "Thus the First World War took on the anguished appearance of a war of exhaustion, a permanent massacre without any great strategic outcome."[3]

As the number of victims rose, it became increasingly difficult to negotiate a peace. The traditional ways of reaching a settlement were inadequate for dealing with the level of violence and the will to sacrifice. The war stopped serving as a "serious means to a serious end," as Clausewitz wanted it to be. In this new situation, the end grew more and more radical to keep up with the means that had unconsciously been released. "Is it passion that arouses technological excessiveness or technological excessiveness that arouses passion?" asked Raymond Aron, who then answered his own question:

> While there was interaction between the two, it is technology, without question or qualification, that is the moving force in this period. Technology prescribed organized bursts of enthusiasm, condemned to failure attempts to reconciliate differences, rejected old forms of diplomatic wisdom and fanned the fires of a crusade mentality. It was technology that led to a peace while creating the conditions for the Second World War.[4]

As time went on, the war freed itself simultaneously from the epic and political models of warfare that until then had been fighting over the definition. Taking leave of Ulysses and Clausewitz, it bade farewell as well to Achilles and Péguy, evading time-honored strategies of combat and measures of achievement. When it was over, no memorial could bear witness more painfully to the radical novelty of this new kind of war than the Tomb of the Unknown Soldier.

Making war and making a name have been tied to each other since ancient times. With combat comes the moment of truth when a name proves its worth. In exposing himself to the greatest danger of all, man distinguishes himself, makes a name for himself, or shows that he deserves his name. Demonstrating bravery and contempt for death guarantees the hero undying fame. Achilles chose a short and glorious life over a long and comfortable one in order not to lose his place in posterity. Hector did the same: "But now death is upon me," he exclaimed. "Let me not die without a struggle, inglorious, but let me do something big, that men to come shall know of it."[5]

Whether they fight for one side or the other, be they Greeks or Trojans, those whose names gain immortality are worthy men. All major achievements applauded today, no matter how peaceful, depend on the luster borrowed from images of war. Great feats are not always feats of arms, but the way we speak of greatness has its origins in war: the first event that detached the individual from the crowd, tore life away from anonymity, and made death unforgettable was the exploits of the warrior in battle.

To honor those who died in combat during World War I required a monument. But since the nature and magnitude of death had changed, a stone could no longer preserve an individual's fame anymore than a lyre; it could only ratify and reify his disappearance with numbers. Born of this unprecedented war, the cult of the unknown soldier was the offspring of two antinomic modes of being that had been defined in opposition to one another since there were wars and men: heroism and the absence of human character, glory, and obscurity. "The virtue of the Unknown Soldier," wrote Ernst Jünger, "is in the fact that he can be replaced, that behind the one killed is the next one in line, already there in reserve."[6]

The discovery and celebration of this virtue canceled out the sense of community that Lussu, and even Jünger, experienced in the trenches. At the front you might see that the enemy was another man, but in the end 870,000 men died. Under this "formidable pressure of the incalculable"[7] and knowledge that those who disappeared would be re-

placed, every man—friend or foe—lost his unique character. In the
process he suffered an unprecedented devaluation, one that perhaps
could not be remedied. "In another time, before the Great War, in the
period when the events related in these pages took place, the life or
death of a man was not yet a matter of indifference," wrote Joseph
Roth at the beginning of chapter 8 of his majestic nostalgic novel *The
Radetzky March*. "When somebody disappeared from the world of the
living, another did not take his place immediately allowing the dead
one to be forgotten. An emptiness remained where he was missed and
witnesses from far and near felt ill at ease when they became aware of
the emptiness."[8]

This very great war filled the void and took Renan at his word, creating an image of the "soldier lost in the immense army advancing to
conquer the perfect." The exalted metaphor became common fate, a
terrible and almost universal condition. Individuals counted for
nothing as war, not science, declared: "Who is this man who places
himself between me and humanity? Why should I care about the insignificant syllables of his name? The name itself is a lie. . . .
Anonymity is far more expressive and true."[9] In affirming the preeminence of the march of humanity over the flesh and blood of individual human beings, the idea of progress returned to history. With
it returned to the world below the great metaphysical division of
being between a lesser reality and a true reality, making this abstract
division concrete and letting it be seen in all its cruelty.

Hence the existential repudiation by artilleryman Franz Rosenzweig of all forms of dualism in philosophy. In the first lines of *The
Star of Redemption*, a work written on postcards in the Balkan
trenches, Rosenzweig wrote:

Let man creep like a worm into the folds of the naked earth
before the fast-approaching volleys of a blind and pitiless
death; let him sense there, forcibly, inexorably, what he otherwise never senses: that his *I* would be but an *It* if he died; let
him therefore cry his very *I* out with every cry that is still in
his throat against the merciless one from whom there is no ap-

peal and who threatens man with such unthinkable annihilation. In the face of all this misery, philosophy only smiles its vacuous smile.[10]

The smile of ancient cosmology. The smile of medieval theology. The smile of Renan, the smile of Hegel who sees Reason "plant the sign of sovereignty on all the mountain tops and in all the valleys." The smile of Marx when he compares the god of history with the "horrible pagan god who drinks nectar only from the skulls of his victims." The metaphysical smile of war that strikes with stupidity at the lives of individuals and reserves reality for anonymous groups. Rosenzweig denounced this indifferent and reductive smile in the name of the creature who trembles before death in a war that dispels the philosophical charm of the One and the All. "After Reason absorbed everything and proclaimed that from now on it alone exists," continued Rosenzweig elsewhere, "man suddenly discovers that although he has been devoured and digested by philosophy for a long time, he is still there. . . . 'I, who am only ashes and dust,' I, a simple private subject, a first name and a last name . . . I am still there and I philosophize."[11]

When war takes over everything, philosophy turns against totality, against the all-encompassing order that it has itself established, against its own indomitability. Rosenzweig challenged the image of self-abnegation that leads man to disappear in the great machine that Jünger celebrated. The artilleryman-philosopher contrasted incarnation and individuation with the terror of an "I, I, I" that is no longer of epic proportions but shaking with anxiety for his place here below, huddled in the entrails or cavities of the earth. He rebelled against history conceived of as an adventure of Reason, an achievement of the universal, as humanity fulfilling itself. For Rosenzweig, the idea of historical Reason came to an end on the battlefield. It died with the war or, rather, with having found in this exaggerated war its grotesque apotheosis.

"We later civilizations . . . we too now know that we are mortal," observed Paul Valéry in *Variété* in 1919.[12] With these solemn words, he marked the caesura and took note, as Rosenzweig did, of the separation between the period inaugurated by the bloody catastrophe and the century of history. Coming out of the Great War, he could no longer assert calmly that the real is always rational, for the irrational itself is necessary for realizing Reason. The dialectic gets stuck, or even unstuck, offering no visible or hidden explanation for the rage of national passions. Reason itself seems to lose its reason, compromising civilization and culture in the abstract ferocity of the battles of weapons and storms of steel. To Renan's cry from the heart: "I who am cultured, I do not find any evil in me,"[13] Valéry retorted with despair:

> So many horrors could not have been possible without so many virtues. Doubtless, much science was needed to kill so many, to waste so much property, annihilate so many cities in so short a time; but *moral qualities* in like number were also needed. Are Knowledge and Duty, then suspect?[14]

The optimism of the Enlightenment was now no longer acceptable even in the form modified by Hegel, who complicated and stripped it of innocence. The war that had just ended prevented one from believing in the promise of progress and in the reality of a prodigious expansion of human abilities and knowledge. Instead of horror serving as an instrument of virtue, virtue now served as an instrument of horror; instead of Reason governing the world with insanity, barbarism now mobilized the resources of Reason and the inventions of science. In the process, civilized Europe wreaked havoc on European civilization while claiming to fulfill its historic mission.

The idea of historical Reason did not die for everyone. Valéry and Rosenzweig could proclaim all they wanted, one in a slightly bombastic tone, the other in a feverish pitch, about how the world war had destroyed history's claim that it had made sense out of human experience. No matter how loud they cried, they were shouting in the desert—not that Europeans were insensitive or unshakable or that they had forgotten about the great massacre. But the rebellion that took place against the war only reinforced, even idealized, history. That is the great misfortune of our century. As Hannah Arendt wrote:

> The days before and the days after the First World War are separated not like the end of an old and the beginning of a new period, but like the day before and the day after an explosion. Yet this figure of speech is as inaccurate as are all others, because the quiet of sorrow which settles down after a catastrophe has never come to pass. The first explosion seems to have touched off a chain reaction in which we have been caught ever since and which nobody seems to be able to stop.[15]

The first reaction in this endless chain was the Russian Revolution.

World War I created the conditions for the Bolsheviks to take power. As they seized the Winter Palace in 1917, the revolutionaries cried out against war, thereby giving their act its universal character. From the moment hostilities broke out in Petrograd, the men fighting in the October Revolution denounced the "social chauvinism" of the Second International as having "symbolized, after the event, the truths and goals betrayed in August 1914."[16] With the Russian Revolution, socialists who had sacrificed their ideas in defense of their countries could now take revenge by turning against the idol of patriotism. After four years of carnage, this coup d'état in a distant place provided socialists, led astray by the dream of adventure or national propaganda, with the opportunity to redeem themselves and to find a positive way out of feeling a sense of disgust or remorse. The light rising in the East had the unexpected brilliance of meaning. The war gave birth to revolution that, in turn, made sense of the meaningless carnage, giving it a double purpose: an occasion to express deserved pity and a warning of the devastation to come. The good news following the war was that the cataclysm could be reintegrated into the history of Reason. The great day of October tore away the long slaughter from the hidden shadows of night and made it possible to examine in the light of day. Don't cry, Valéry! Lenin said, "Capitalist society has always been a horror without end and it remains so. If the present war, therefore, the most reactionary of all wars, prepares this society for an end filled with horrors, we have no reason to despair."[17] We others, members of barbaric civilizations, we know that we must die in order to make room for true civilization.

Not everyone was as blunt as Lenin. Still the fact remains that Rosenzweig was wrong: instead of entering a post-Hegelian era, the twentieth century had fallen firmly into the clutches of Hegelianism, of a Hegelianism, moreover, that was no longer contemplative, inspired by the glow of twilight, but by the light of the morning, unrestrained and militant. History collapsed in 1914 only to rise again in 1917 as historicism, with such seductive force that it had the power to mystify and destroy at a level never attained before. The image of the new good was painfully born, and it obscured all feelings of disaster.

Thus the smile of philosophy did not disappear with the protest of individuals or, as Rosenzweig predicted, "with the private subject, a last name and a first name"; instead, it froze into a cruel grin on the countless faces of those who sacrificed their scruples to the Angel of Reason and gained never ending strength from the certainty that they were speeding up the meaning of history. Shaken by the war, the idea of a reasonable universe was guaranteed by the revolution. If one could now say that philosophy was finished, it was not because the concept of being had escaped its grip, but the opposite. Philosophy had merged with reality. The real and the rational, once tentatively imagined as possibly being different, now came together in the grandiose spectacle of a redemptive fairy tale. The catastrophe of history gave life to the concept of history, and faith in this concept made the catastrophe worse and eclipsed it at the same time. This is the founding irony of the century.

To this another paradox is added, another painful irony. The prestige and influence of Lenin in 1918 were based in large part on his radical pacifism. But while he may have turned the revolution against the war, Lenin, whose laugh the Capri fisherman had appreciated, fashioned his idea and practice of revolution on the model of war—and not just any war, but *this* war.

Lenin admired Clausewitz, but he got him wrong: "War is not a mere act of policy," proclaimed the great Prussian officer in his famous phrase "but a true political instrument, a continuation of politics through other means."[18] In other words, the belligerent act is not an isolated act. Commerce between nations does not stop entirely when the guns go off. The violent phase inserts itself into an ongoing situation, serving purposes and interests beyond military logic. That is why laws pushing armies to violent extremes do not generally guide military conflicts—do not generally, perhaps, but, as we have just seen, they did in the case of 1914. This war tricked its protagonists. Having departed on a "fresh and joyous" expedition, nations found themselves trapped in an endless conflict that required the total mobilization of populations and industries. A total war demands an absolute victory: "disarming the enemy and achieving a dictated rather than negotiated peace became the highest goal of the war."[19] What occurred was what Clausewitz told us would occur if combat were no longer guided by the "will of a leading intelligence": war would take the place of policy, becoming "its own independent will," "a complete, untrammeled, absolute manifestation of violence." War would "usurp the place of policy the moment policy brought it into being; it would then drive policy out of office and rule by the laws of its own nature, very much like a mine that can explode only in the manner or direction predetermined by the setting."[20]

Even as he laid claim to Clausewitz and ceaselessly denounced this imperialist war, Lenin reversed the Prussian strategist's dogma and pushed his own interpretation to the limit. For Lenin, war free of politics became the essence of politics itself. He saw class struggle as breaking the last links that, for Marx, still attached war to classical forms of hostility or disagreement. Now it became a manifestation of absolute violence, a strategy for annihilation taken to the extreme. In another time the military enemy had a political reality, but Lenin's political enemy was nothing more than the object of a military will for destruction:

> Social priests and opportunists are always ready to dream about a pacifist socialism of the future, but what distinguishes them

from revolutionary social democrats is that they do not want to imagine or think about the bitter class struggle and class warfare necessary in order to bring about this magnificent future.[21]

A new period had begun in which political involvement meant taking up arms, not merely participating in the public sphere. In this climate, the activist takes sides by becoming a soldier, and the intellectual uses words as his weapon, compensating as best he can for the weaknesses of language. To fight unto death is the guiding motto for building both speech and action. Acclaimed for his pacifism, Lenin turned peacetime conflicts into brutal encounters, relying heavily on the radical quality and inherent excesses of total war. The revolution takes on the form of the very war it denounces. Its ambition is to crush the enemy, its ideal an army unit in marching order.

"Let us take the modern army," Lenin instructed in *The Bankruptcy of the Second International*, a text devoted to analyzing social chauvinism:

> Here is a good example of organization. This organization is good not only because it is flexible, but because it gives millions of men a single purpose. Today these millions of men are at home in the four corners of the country. Tomorrow they receive the order to mobilize and they gather at specified rallying points. Today they are in the trenches, sometimes for months. Tomorrow, grouped differently, they attack. Today they perform wonders, while sheltering themselves from bullets and shrapnel. Tomorrow they perform wonders while fighting unprotected. Today their advanced detachment dig mine furnaces under ground; tomorrow they pick up stakes and move a distance of tens of versts, following instructions of pilots circling the earth. Yes, this is what organization means, when, with the same purpose in mind, millions of men change the form of their relations and of their actions, change the place where their activity occurs and the way they do it, change their instruments, according to the specific circumstances and needs of the struggle.[22]

Total chaos falls into a huge battalion; the noisy crowd, into an impressively harmonious and homogeneous structure. Uncontrollable multitudes take the shape of a multiform being, manageable and disciplined. That is how humanity appears in a total war, in which existence is converted into energy and every individual—in the factory and on the front—is reduced to being part of the machine, a bit of willpower, a cog in the wheel. When political movements raise this specter as their highest value, we call them *totalitarian*. And this is what Leninism did with its "Down with war! Long live the army!" So did National Socialism.

The trauma of defeat in Germany made it possible for the extreme right to convince many people to accept the modern image of the enemy and reject the traditional theme of a fallen humanity. Humiliated by the Versailles Treaty, Germans began reading *The Protocols of the Elders of Zion* in increasing numbers and seeing it as a revelation. "In Berlin I attended several meetings which were entirely devoted to *The Protocols*," wrote a Jewish observer.

> The speaker was usually a professor, a teacher, an editor, a lawyer or someone of that kind. The audience consisted of members of the educated class, civil servants, tradesmen, former officers, ladies, above all students, students of all faculties and years of seniority. . . . Passions were whipped up to a boiling-point. There, in front of us, in the flesh, was the cause of all our ills—the one who had made the war, brought about the defeat and engineered the revolution; the one who had conjured up all our suffering. This enemy was quite close by; he could be caught with our hands. And yet this same enemy could slink about in the dark; one shuddered to think what secret designs he was harbouring.[23]

Since their military commanders never proclaimed defeat, the Germans learned that they had lost the war "in full victory" while believing that their troops still formed a continuous front in Belgium and France. *The Protocols*, therefore, confirmed the "stabbing-in-the-back" thesis at just the right time. It announced who struck down the Germans and who was guilty of signing the armistice on November 9, 1918, when Germany was still "unconquered on the battlefield." "It is then," Hitler confided in *Mein Kampf*, "that my hatred for the authors of these events was born," and the "Unknown Soldier of the Great War," as he liked to call himself, chose the very same day in 1938 to burn down synagogues and Jewish stores throughout Germany. Now Führer of his people, Hitler picked November 9 to give his response to the assassination of the third secretary of the German embassy in Paris. His response, as we know, was called Kristallnacht.

The indignity of 1918 thus erased the "ideas of 1914." The war in Germany could no longer claim to represent the struggle between the principle of the French Revolution and the trinity of order, duty, and justice. Now it justified itself as a response to a global enemy, as the exaltation of strength and the ideology of will.

The war also had another antireactionary effect on antidemocratic thought. Once the hostilities subsided, nostalgia sprung up, assuming an absolutely unrecognizable form. For those who went through it, the experience on the front became a new lost treasure, a new political horizon. Brotherhood in the trenches replaced the ties soldiers had before the war, in the village and on the farm.

Suffering from the dissolving effects of civil life, the soldiers rebelled against their unhappy isolation and looked for ways to return and strengthen the loosening ties of communitarian life. To make their case, they contrasted *Gemeinschaft*—the concrete community, organic and authentic, substantial and living—with *Gesellschaft*—bourgeois society, cold, mechanical, and abstract. Based entirely on contract, everything in the *Gesellschaft* followed a proscribed method, excluding all that was not calculation, allowing personal self-interest to define the terms of all human relations. But the concrete community they had in mind resembled a battlefield, not the preindustrial countryside. Even the wheat fields had been modernized by the memory of the war. There was no longer anything bucolic in the evocation, nothing Virgil-like in the hymn, nothing backward looking in the enthusiasm expressed in the verses. In his book on the worker (*Der Arbeiter*), Ernst Jünger wrote:

> A field cultivated and fertilized with industrial nitrates from factories is no longer the same field. It is therefore not true that existence is timeless and that great transformations pass over plowed fields like the wind and the clouds. The impact of the revolution that is sweeping us along is demonstrated precisely in the way it breaks up old states.[24]

The counterrevolution disappears into the idea of revolution when the cult of technology replaces the cult of the countryside— even in the countryside—which is exactly what happened after World War I. As George Orwell observed in 1941, one could no longer distinguish between the two after 1914. Still, people continued to celebrate "a series of victories won by scientific man over the romantic man" and to call these victories historical progress.[25] Throughout the nineteenth century and the beginning of the twentieth, "society was ruled by narrow-minded, profoundly incurious people, predatory businessmen, dull squires, bishops, politicians who could quote Horace but had never heard of algebra. Science was faintly disreputable and religious belief obligatory. Traditionalism, stupidity, snobbishness, patriotism, superstition and love of war seemed to be all on the same side."[26] World War I had changed all that, explained Orwell, but many progressives followed the example of H. G. Wells, the most famous English intellectual of the period, and still believed in the

> supposed antithesis between the man of science who is working towards a planned World State and the reactionary who is trying to restore a disorderly past. . . . On the one side science, order, progress, internationalism, aeroplanes, steel, concrete, hygiene; on the other side war, nationalism, religion, monarchy, peasants, Greek professors, poets, horses.[27]

With this line of reasoning, Orwell continued, H.G. Wells, the author of *The Time Machine* and a firm opponent of glorified renderings of days of yore, dismissed Hitler as "an absurdity, a ghost from the past, a creature doomed to disappear almost immediately."[28] With unshakable optimism, H.G. Wells joined others of the World War I era in equating science and common sense and in not seeing, in the words of Orwell, that Nazi Germany was "far more scientific than England, and far more barbarous."[29] Scientific and barbarous: that is the definition of a state that, in times of peace and in times of war, turns every individual into a piece of machinery and encourages everyone to embrace the destiny of the Unknown Soldier as a universal vocation.

Achieving everything while fighting: nostalgia and hope come together in a totalitarian surge forward, creating a regime in which all men merge into one. In a world like this, concluded Hannah Arendt in the final pages of her great reflection: "Men insofar as they are more than animal reaction and fulfillment of functions are entirely superfluous to totalitarian regimes. Totalitarianism strives not *toward despotic rule over men, but toward a system in which men are superfluous.*"[30]

Under totalitarianism, concentration camps may not be economically useful, but they are ontologically necessary. To make sure that a single purpose reigns, it is necessary to liquidate the enemy of man while liquidating in man all his spontaneity, singularity, and unpredictability—all that makes a human being's character unique. In this system, death factories become humanity factories without humans. Reconstructing the idea of a radical utopia and extreme politics, the purpose of these factories is to annihilate the adversary *physically* while making the many disappear *metaphysically* into the one. "Society believes it is alone, but someone is there," wrote Artaud magnificently. "As long as someone is there, humanity is imperfect," proclaims concentration-camp socialism of all stripes. Thus two types of cadavers are produced: dead cadavers and living ones, these "marionettes with human faces,"[31] this anonymous replaceable mass, these people-less people in whom the divine light has gone out, these beings without faces described by Primo Levi as crowding his memory: "If I could sum up all the evil of our time with a single image, I would use one that is very familiar to me: an emaciated man, his head bowed, his shoulders stooped, whose face and eyes give no sign of thinking."[32]

A tiredness so heavy that the instinct to survive gives up the struggle. This tiredness lacks even the strength necessary to say "I" in the face of a pitiless death. Varlam Shalamov has described it in *Kolyma Tales*. The great narrator of the other camp experience tells the story of young Dougaïev who was ordered to dig up rocks. Although he tried very hard to perform his task well, Dougaïev did not measure up. One day, after the prisoners were allowed to stop for the night, the soldiers led him away to kill him: "When he realized what was happening, Dougaïev was sorry he had worked so hard, that he had suffered for nothing on his very last day."[33]

Using an unfortunate phrase by Adorno, which the philosopher himself later retracted, some people still ask whether poetry can exist after Auschwitz. Expressed out of despair at the end of the war, the phrase has evolved into something fashionable to say, an automatic reflex, justifying interminable discussions about the breakdown of culture in Auschwitz or the silence of those who returned from the camps. In the face of those claiming it cannot be done, survivors, blessed with literary genius, feel compelled to record their stories. They have to speak, they tell us, less out of an autobiographical need to bear witness for what they had personally endured than out of a sort of *heterobiographical* obligation to bear witness for others, for those who disappeared, in order to save them from their anonymous fate. No matter how hostile their efforts may be to aesthetic forms, the urgency they feel to give to the dead a narrative voice recreates poetry. As Solzhenitsyn so admirably observed, the only substitute for experiencing what one has not actually lived is art, literature: "Making up for man's scant time on earth, art transmits between men the entire accumulated load of another being's life experience, with all its hardships, colors, and juices. It recreates—life-like—the experience of other men, so that we can assimilate it as our own."[34] Thus we must reverse Adorno's formula: without art, that is, without poetry, the possibility of understanding what went on in Auschwitz or Kolyma would be closed to us forever.

Primo Levi's story of little Hurbinek is exemplary:

Hurbinek was a nobody, a child of death, a child of Auschwitz. He looked maybe three years old, no one knew anything about him, he could not speak and he had no name; that curious name, Hurbinek, had been given to him by us, perhaps by one of the women who used these syllables to give shape to the inarticulate sounds the child sometimes made. He was paralyzed from the waist down, with atrophied legs, thin like sticks; but his eyes, lost in a triangular and wasted face, flashed, terribly alive, full of demand, assertion, of the will to break loose and shatter the tomb of his dumbness. The speech he lacked, which no one had bothered to teach him, this need for speech charged his stare with explosive urgency: it was a stare both savage and human, even mature, a judgement which none of us could support, so heavy was it with force and anguish.[35]

After the Red Army liberated Auschwitz, Levi ended up in an infirmary, together with Hurbinek and countless other sick people. There, Hurbinek succeeded in saying a word, something like "Massklo" or "Matisklo." Was this his name? What was he saying? Surrounded, though he was, by representatives of every nation in Central Europe, Hurbinek's utterance did not reveal its secret. And so:

Hurbinek who was not yet three years old, who was, perhaps, born in Auschwitz and never saw a tree, Hurbinek who fought like a man till his very last breath to gain entry into the community of men from which a bestial power had excluded him; Hurbinek, the nameless one, whose tiny forearm—even his—bore the tattoo of Auschwitz, died in the first days of March 1945; free but not redeemed. Nothing remains of him: he only bears witness through my words.[36]

Hurbinek, the child with no origin or language, was destined to die a death that was itself indifferent and without words. No trace of his time on earth was meant to be preserved. The account in *The Reawakening* foils the plan: nothing, it is true, remains of the child who was nobody but the words with which Primo Levi tells his story, giving this inarticulate dead child his singular body and expression. These few words offer a rough sketch of the life that was his, his humanity—his unique character that could not be substituted for another. Hurbinek did not have enough time to become a man or even to have a verbal existence, but he was already "a special individual, a person, a unique being, irreparable, that nothing else will replace." Michelet's epitaph for the duke of Orleans, assassinated by the people of Burgundy, also fits this child without a name, dead at the age of three in Auschwitz: "Nothing like him before, nothing like him after; God will not begin again. Others will come along, no doubt; the world does not tire, other people will follow, perhaps better ones, but not the same, never, never."[37]

All the same—that is, human; each one different—that is, in themselves; together men form a community of exceptions in the world. In the camps, it was just the opposite: an experiment to fuse individuals into a compact and anonymous totality; to recognize nothing that distinguishes one man from another. Packing people into cattle cars, beating them, starving them, depriving them of speech, shaving their heads, tattooing numbers on their arms—everything is done to eliminate the unique identity of everyone so that all that remains of man is his affiliation with a single human species.

Varlam Shalamov and Primo Levi reversed the process in their memoirs. Meticulous narrators and tireless smugglers of refugees, they returned to the world those people they knew in the concentration camp. They restored qualities to each that went beyond what made them simple examples of the type or species, even if this transcendence was nothing more than a desperate fight, as it was for Hurbinek, to enter the circle of human conversation.

five

Humanitarian Amends

WE WILL UNDERSTAND NOTHING about the evil of the twentieth century if we think it scandalous, *a priori*, to compare National Socialism and Stalinist Communism. Nor will we understand anything about it, if we take the totalitarian relationship as given.

Aleksander Wat was born in Poland on May 1, 1900. In the days following the Great War this futurist poet, admired by Mayakovsky, enthusiastically joined the Communist Party, inspired by two dreams: artistic freedom and social justice. "The star of Communism is new, new, new," he could have said, together with the Czech novelist Vladislav Vančura, and then added, "there is no modernity beyond it."[1]

Hence the shock, pain, and confusion when the poet discovered similarities in the early 1930s between a system considered the antithesis of European humanism and one striving to be its fulfillment. In *My Century*, his magnificent and monumental series of interviews with Czeslaw Milosz, Aleksander Wat questioned himself relentlessly about the abominable mystery of the relationship. In the beginning there was the proverb: "Everyone who went over to Communism had to accept the Leninist principle that you couldn't make omelettes without breaking eggs."[2] This culinary metaphor was supposed to explain the harsh law about the price you must pay. If you want to create a classless society, you will have to use violence and even accept the possibility of making mistakes. But taken literally, the Leninist proverb is more ferocious still: the eggs you break are the fundamental ingredient. They are not simply part of the cost of preparation, nicely compensated for by the omelette itself, like the pot that inevitably cracks when making certain dishes. These eggs are indispensable: the more eggs you break, the better the omelette. In the same spirit, Wat observed, "All that blood spilled for the revolution . . . all the savagery . . . it all worked in favor of Communism. . . . How pure and great must be the cause for which so much blood was spilled, innocent blood. That was terribly attractive."[3]

In 1935, Wat came out from under the spell. The constructivist dizziness lifted. He no longer compared history to the preparation of a dish or people's blood to a kind of material or ingredient. From that time on, Lenin's image of the omelette lost its power to beautify or sanctify the countless horrors of the revolution.

Worried but eager to see things clearly, Wat rushed to the house of the Communist poet Wadyslaw Broniewski, who had just returned from the Soviet Union. Tormented by doubt and remorse, he bombarded Broniewski with questions about the famine in the Ukraine and about collectivization:

> The press had reported that five million peasants had lost their lives. And he said: "Yes, that's right, it's being talked about a lot. . . . " Tretiakov, the author of the play *Cry China*, had told him that something like four or five million people had been annihilated, wiped out. And so I said to Wladzio—I remember this exactly; there are moments in life you don't forget— "So, is it true?" He whisked his hand disparagingly, dismissing the subject; what did those five million *mushiks* mean to him? He didn't say it, but that gesture![4]

Each thing in its time: the agony of the dying classes is part of the plan. The revolution sounds the death knell for the past. Humanity has succeeded and needs no justification. That is the meaning of the disparaging gestures and scornful whistles, the response every revolutionary gets when he does not accept the news from the front with virile terseness—the sort of toughness that separates the men from the boys—or with a look that communicates courage. So it seems that Doktor Pannwitz and his kind are not alone in releasing themselves from the bonds of humanity. Others do the same and for diametrically opposed reasons, not in the name of maintaining the racial superiority of the lords, but of finally realizing the unity of the human species. The ultimate goal matters little. Once history determines what can be made or produced, it exposes men to limitless violence and takes away their ontological dignity.

Men become nothing more than the stones of a gigantic edifice, the means, obstacles, or rough outlines of a masterpiece. In each case, the masterpiece bears a different name—"hierarchy" in one, "equality" in the other. From Pannwitz the engineer to Broniewski the poet, the idea of humanity that we have inherited is both fragile and harmful, mortal and murderous, leaving us with two urgent tasks: to preserve the idea of humanity and to make sure the idea does not kill, so that we might stop comparing humanity to an omelette, stop seeing it as the complement of the object of the verb *to make*. By developing humanitarian sensibilities and humanitarian forms of action, our generation assumes the responsibility of restoring the legacy that Aleksander Wat's century has bequeathed to us.

Everything began in 1968, far away from the barricades and the graffiti, in a region known only to specialists of Africa: Biafra. One year earlier, the Ibos, who were the majority in this southern province of Nigeria, seceded and declared their independence. The central government responded by starting a war and, after taking Port Harcourt, by closing off the territory controlled by the rebels. Despite the horrifying famine that struck the area, threatening the population in this Biafran "hideout"—1 million people died in thirty months—most countries considered progressive supported Nigeria against Biafra and did so without any qualms—Algeria, Nasser's Egypt, Guinea, the Soviet Union. Biafra had the support of South Africa and Portugal, awkward allies at the time. France hesitated: Charles de Gaulle, the great defender of the rights of people to determine their own destiny, had the opportunity to weaken the giant of English-speaking Africa. But loyal to the principle of inviolable borders, he resisted the temptation to topple Nigeria and support the "courageous people of Biafra." Thus he refused to make the decisive gesture and recognize the new nation, for which he expressed a good deal of sympathy; instead, he sent the French Red Cross. The doctors recruited, however, were powerless. Although they received a great deal of assistance for this first major humanitarian operation in a Third World country, the doctors were unable to keep the territory from surrendering in 1970. Strangled and starved, Biafra became a second Solferino.

The story is well known. After witnessing the terrible spectacle on the battlefield of Solferino, the Swiss businessman Henri Dunant decided to create the Red Cross and devote the rest of his life to the organization. Having come to Lombardy on June 25, 1859, to seek permission from Napoleon III to purchase land in Algeria, when he arrived in Solferino, he did not see the emperor, who had already left, but found forty thousand unfortunate souls rotting in the sun:

> Some, mostly those who have been severely wounded, are dazed and seem not to understand what you say to them; they look at you with wild eyes, but this apparent prostration does not prevent them from feeling pain. The others look worried and agitated, trembling convulsively, nerves in shock. Their open wounds are swollen. Twisted, writhing and crazed with pain, they ask us to kill them, their faces contorted in the last grip of agony. Further on we see unfortunate souls who were not only thrown to the ground by bullets or shell fragments, but who then fell under the wheels of the artillery, which rolled over their bodies, crushing their arms and legs.[5]

In Solferino, Henri Dunant discovered how the same war draws soldiers together to fight against one another, then unites the victims from opposing sides through suffering. "Tutti fratelli," said the women of Castiglione, who also understood. They made no distinction among those who had fallen but went onto the field to help everyone, both the wounded Italians and their wounded enemies.

What establishes this sense of brotherhood has nothing to do with those special qualities we traditionally call human or with those qualities, uniquely human once again, that separate man from nature—the capacity to act freely and share a sense of dignity with all beings capable of reason. Rather, brotherhood has its roots in weakness and pain. As the citizen of Geneva noted in *Emile*:

> Men are not naturally kings, or great, or rich. They are all born naked and poor, all subject to the miseries of life, to the sadness, needs and pain of the entire species. In the end, they are all condemned to death. That is what man truly is, from which no mortal is exempt.[6]

In other words, the man in man does not recognize himself by his properties, faculties, or prerogatives but by the torments that overwhelm him. *Ecce homo*, said Rousseau, echoing Pontius Pilate, in the guise of a definition of the human being.

A century later, struggling with these conflicting images of humanity, another man from Geneva, Henri Dunant, proclaimed the need for creating a humane place on the very fields of absolute violence, where all soldiers could fall when they were wounded:

> At the solemn hour when men, fellow citizens, Christians, armed against each other, have just spilled their soldiers' blood on land that should only be soaked with the sweat of their labor, I want charity, in the form of a first aid society, to challenge war for the right to claim victims hit by iron, but not yet reaped by death.[7]

Dunant's wish became reality on August 22, 1864, with the signing of the First Geneva Convention to improve the fate of soldiers at war. With this convention, the International Red Cross came into being, establishing the principle of a double neutrality: it would fulfill its mission and protect all the victims by taking no part in the hostilities and no public stand in favor of one side or the other. This new charitable organization did not care where suffering bodies came from, what uniforms covered them, or what flags represented them. Its authority rested solely on being above all controversies that led to conflict, be they political, philosophical, racial, or religious. In refusing to choose among the unfortunate wounded, it refused to choose among the actors as well and judge the conduct of governments. Charity and silence went hand in hand, but even this compromise was compromised. In accepting the logic of sovereignty, untouchable at the time, Henri Dunant's humanitarian project required the cooperation and goodwill of recognized states.

What a formidable and ambiguous arrangement! Alerted since 1942 to the fate of the Jews and the existence of extermination camps, the International Red Cross said nothing, in order to protect its work with prisoners of war. To gain the cooperation of Nigeria forty years later, the same silent authority gave four times more aid to zones controlled by the federal government than it did to Biafra where famine was ravaging the population.[8]

The French doctors who went to Biafra in 1968 broke with tradition and abandoned caution. They entered foreign territory illegally and, upon returning, testified. Defying the rules of silence in this second Solferino, they called for a new charter of humanitarian organizations:

> Humanitarian aid is in the hands of large organizations run by bureaucrats; we must give those in the field, particularly doctors, the possibility to intervene directly. Humanitarian aid bows to rules and arbitrary authorities that violate the law; we must work only with the victims and have the freedom to bend established regulations when they are used against man. Humanitarian aid is dependent on States; we must free this aid and make it independent by seeking the support of a new force: the media and public opinion.[9]

But these noisy objections and calls for intervention are not acts of treason. While fiercely challenging the discretion and good manners of the Red Cross, they remain faithful to its commitment to neutrality. Facing the contempt of revolutionaries—real or imaginary—these doctors were defending the great timeless principles that inspired

Dunant, the naive universalism of the organization's moral code. In the process, they challenged those who claim to have all the answers, who smile with conviction upon hearing that the *mushiks* have been annihilated or seeing images of Biafran children with swollen stom- achs. This new humanitarian generation joined Dunant in proclaiming the right and duty to help every victim no matter what camp history places him in or what ideological sign his oppressor falls under.

The ways of the Lord are unworkable: we question God less and Providence more, in both the religious and secular forms that modern man has given to them. We refuse to accept violence as part of a plan that encompasses everybody or reconcile evil in the name of humanity. Thus we no longer say, with Trotsky, that the most savage acts are commendable if done to bring about equality or that the most merciful acts are despicable if they delay or hinder the definitive and universal rise of moral standards.[10] We affirm instead, together with Lévinas, that "justifying the pain of my neighbor is the source of all immorality."[11] We are not afraid to dirty our hands. Overcoming our revulsion, we plunge them right into the excrement and blood, in order to put lives crushed by history back together again and prevent further destruction. We no longer divide the wounded into those on the right and those on the left.

In contrast to the internationalist whose cause in the past he sometimes championed (and for whose cynical idealism he now atones), the rescuer without borders embraces all silent calls of distress, subjecting them to no preliminary cross-examination. Instead of questioning first impulses, he follows his instincts, precisely because it is the good thing to do; instead of working for the cause, he gives in to his feelings. Historical reason was used to stifle sentimental reason. Now the heart, not history, guides the way, giving emotions their rights once again. And so after a long digression with Marx, Hegel, and their human omelette, the idea of humanity rejects its culinary destiny. Bidding good-bye to the nineteenth century at the end of the twentieth, the idea of humanity returns to Rousseau.

Humanitarian man gives in to pity when he starts seeing his neighbors' throats being cut right under his own window—and watches this occur in every corner of the globe, thanks to the ubiquity of television, that incalculable event that invades the homes of people all over the world. In the process, he releases himself from the hold of the philosopher, about whom Rousseau, predicting the future, sarcastically noted in his *Discourse on the Origin of Inequality*: "Nothing can [disturb the tranquil sleep of the philosopher or] tear him from his bed but such general evils as threaten the whole community."[12] Continuing in the same critical tone, Rousseau added that "man has only to put his hands to his ears and argue a little with himself, to prevent nature, which he has shocked within him, from identifying itself with the unfortunate sufferer." Today, be he doctor, pharmacist, nurse, engineer, escort, or even simple spectator, humanitarian man no longer argues with himself but abandons himself. Having freed himself from the selective and abstract altruism imposed on him by the movement of history, he is now "rashly ready to obey the first promptings of humanity."[13]

Who would dare criticize this rashness? Who would have the heart to reject the Rousseau-like affirmation of Michel Foucault— "The misfortunes of men must never become the silent left-overs of politics"[14]—in favor of a politics based on astounding dialectical thinking that successfully turned evil into an instrument of good and good into a force that was objectively dangerous?

Under these circumstances, there is no way to feel sorry that the general mood at the end of the century is a little rasher and a little less stunning. There is no way to question an intrusive and noisy humanitarianism that has simultaneously toppled Swiss regulations for administering pity and the pitiless philosophy of history. But there is no feeling of triumph, either. The global doctor is as reductive in his thinking as the political activist. Where the activist sees men playing their role in the drama of reason, the global doctor sees victims of misery and sickness.

The activist asks whose side the wounded are on and when they joined the struggle. Are they progressive or reactionary? Did they suffer for the right or wrong reasons? For the activist, there is only historical reality. No price is too high to threaten his sense of solidarity or tempt him to wander off the superhighway of history. The global doctor, on the other hand, may have no agenda, but that does not mean he cares very much either about who the suffering individual is—about his being or his reason for being, the world he wants to build, the causes of his persecution and suffering, the meaning he gives to his history and perhaps to his death. Save lives: that is the global mission of the global doctor. He is too busy feeding rice to hungry mouths to listen to what these mouths are saying. Words do not concern him. He turns his attention to murdered populations, not to eloquent voices, to the transparent language of complaint, not the opaque tongues of individual nations. The bodies he cares for are disembodied. "Water! Water!"—this primitive cry is what passes for *logos* today, the cry of an undifferentiated mass of humanity.

"In the infirmary," observed Michel Serres quite correctly, "the suffering and moaning of everyone is the same. Like violence and death, pain is universal; it makes us all equal. The same bitterness pours salt on sweat, tears and blood."[15] But in response to the author of *Angels, a Modern Myth*, who bases his moral system on this kind of social leveling, Goethe noted in 1787, "I must admit that I too consider it true that humanity will finally be victorious, but I also fear that the world will turn into a vast hospital and each of us will become the other's humane nurse."[16] To which Bernanos, who is closer to us in time, added:

> No matter how many times we review the history of the world, we never find people who love pitiful souls for themselves. The more fortunate put up with or tolerate the wretched out of pity. And by pitying them, they exclude them from love, for love obeys the law of reciprocity and pity makes reciprocity impossible. Pity is fallen love, debased, a thin trickle of holy water disappearing into the sand.[17]

Furthermore, despite appearances to the contrary, pity does not exclude feelings of misanthropy. What looks at first like a positive gesture, to include everyone by reducing all human bonds to a single sense of humanity, turns out in the end to be motivated less by a concern for others than by an invincible mistrust of individual human freedom.

Let us be very clear: we know that a doctor would break his medical vows if he did not attend to every patient who came in, without stopping to consider his opinions, projects, or place of origin. When the healer without borders proclaims emphatically: "I promise to care, to the best of my abilities, for those suffering around the world in either mind or body," we can only rejoice in his expression of fidelity to medical ethics and his commitment to modernize the Hippocratic oath, adapting it to contemporary images of the global village. Things break down, however, when we start looking at the world with the eyes of a doctor, when our interest in others focuses mainly on saving lives, and when suffering people, unable to rise and speak for themselves, gain our sympathy for being, as Régis Debray put it, "the target of any place and of anything,"[18] and for nothing more. Things break down when, with our eyes completely open, we can no longer see the difference between accident and aggression and describe the multiplicity of catastrophes with the same narrative theme, as interchangeable victims, as "Martians belonging to nowhere, ending up in this place instead of that, without any reason, by the vagaries of chance."[19]

With so many causes betrayed, so many crimes committed in the name of higher values—in particular, humanity—it is certainly legitimate to want to climb down from the lofty heights and attend to the urgent matters at hand. If this infernal century has taught us anything, it is to bid earthly paradise farewell. Better to fight evil wherever it appears than to set one's sights on a hypothetical good and enter into the murderous dialectic of means and ends in the hopes of attaining it.

We cannot, however, trace the popularity of humanitarian feelings to the loss of affection for great promises. It owes its global success to its reductive simplicity and attraction to causes that can do no wrong. How can we refuse the "boat people" a safe haven? Expelled and famished, they are dependent and afflicted, suffering and in need. They are not active beings who cannot be controlled.

The humanitarian generation wants to bring to an end the age of ideology that subjected the history of men to the logic of a single idea. But it continues to think ideologically, refusing to expose itself to the "infinitely improbable" which, to use once again an expression of Hannah Arendt's, constitutes the "very texture of the real." The humanitarian generation does not like men—they are too disconcerting—but enjoys taking care of them. Free men scare it. Eager to express tenderness fully while making sure that men do not get away, it prefers handicapped people. Recently misled by the myth of human progress, it now falls back on the indisputable truth about suffering humanity, thus avoiding all bad surprises. No longer susceptible to the grand scheme of history, it is only interested in the misfortune of the species. Its sense of solidarity takes the shape of a great caregiving operation.

Attending to anonymous people in desperate situations, the humanitarian generation is motivated by principles of caution, not brotherly love. Expressing a sense of extreme moral urgency while enjoying the comfort of great moral security, it exchanges its mission of surpassing history for one of infallibility. With unshaking confidence that it can do no wrong, this generation has turned off the sound on the cries of misery, on an uncertain and complicated humanity. No need to listen, for the will to live is simple. Victims call out in a single voice and that voice does not lie.

As Paul Ricoeur wrote:

> Horror attaches to events that must never be forgotten. It constitutes the ultimate ethical motivation of the history of victims. (I prefer to say the history of victims rather than the history of the vanquished, for the vanquished are, in part, candidates for domination who failed.) The victims of Auschwitz are the representatives, par excellence, in our memory of all history's victims. Victimization is the other side of history that no trick of reason can ever justify. It reveals instead the scandal of every theodicy of history.[20]

Humanitarians get credit for having denounced the scandal and rehabilitated the victim. "In earthquakes or social upheavals, every victim is first and foremost somebody 'to be saved,'"[21] observed André Glucksmann. But who, precisely, is the victim? This is not at all clear: a man separated from his surroundings, uprooted, forced to leave his land and his situation, feeling empty, deprived of opportunities, all thanks to a nameless misfortune. It is not man in the singular who lives on this earth, but men in their infinite diversity, Hannah Arendt liked to say. Yet given the ongoing temptation to reduce men to Man, she found herself having to drive the point home on innumerable occasions. Yesterday, this temptation took the heroic form of ideology; today it triumphs in the form of solicitude. With ideology it was the progress of man that put an end to human beings in the plural; with solicitude, it is the species man and the anonymous tribulations of his representatives. In the age of ideology, we believed we knew everything; in the age of doing good, we want to know nothing.

This change encompasses everything, but it is not a revolution. From establishing happiness definitively on Earth to fighting all forms of inhumanity, from the primacy of reason to that of feeling—we find the same intolerance, the same resentment in the face of weakness and unpredictability, in the face of what the Greeks used to call human affairs. There is just as much political conspiracy at work when we compare conflicts between men to natural cataclysms as there is when we liken the hope for universal freedom to a total march forward. The other side of compassion rebels against the risk that human beings pose to all forms of judgment by their diversity and by presenting themselves as a permanent riddle. In becoming humanitarian, man has not given up his claim to the comprehensive insurance policy that ideology promised to him. He is just using it differently to escape certain practical problems, but he still fully intends to cash in.

At the end of "a century which, in sixty years, has seen two world wars, totalitarianism on the right and the left, Hitlerism and Stalinism, Hiroshima, the Gulag, the genocides of Auschwitz and Cambodia,"[22] we can no longer explain or pacify evil by incorporating it into a plan of the whole. Lévinas and Ricoeur stated this forcefully. Our century is the century of useless suffering and, as such, does not look for dialectical motivations, but for soothing interventions, free of all *a prioris*, made immediately and whenever possible. But this blinkerless new philanthropy presents problems as well, given its close ties to the horror. Having learned the lesson of our century, the new philanthropy refuses to remain outside the humanitarian space of catastrophe. Moved only by big calamities, unquestionable disasters, and passive distress, it needs blood—and a lot of it—to go into action. When all is said and done, it may be just as cruel to respond to the misery of the world with sentimental alienation as it is with the virile exercise of the trick of reason.

We cannot even be sure that humanitarian solutions are less blind. God sees clearly, but in the beautiful phrase of Milan Kundera, "man proceeds in the fog."[23] Fog is his fate, even when he thinks he is living under the sun of reason or the honest light of feeling, even when the experience of being is presented to him as a complete picture or when he reaches out to unfortunate souls without being selective. Joining the humanitarian side and supporting the victims does not mean, despite appearances, that we have made the right choice. No matter what we do, it is risky and uncertain. Commitment is always a gamble, no matter how carefully we have thought about it. This remains true even when the image of suffering is everywhere and opinion obliges the General Assembly of the United Nations to turn the law of humanitarian aid into international law.

On December 8, 1988, the world saw Dunant's dream come true in the very sanctuary of sovereignty, with the affirmation of the right of access to the victims. But this dream was short lived, as the humanitarian escort has witnessed in the last conflict of this century on European soil—the war for Greater Serbia that began in Kosovo in 1989 and concluded [temporarily] in the final months of 1995 with a very precarious peace in Bosnia-Herzegovina. Once again, the logic of the state rapidly took over. Using the new media style, it was easy

to hide the coldest calculations of self-interest or powerless will behind the uplifting show of good intentions and humanitarian aid.
Rony Brauman offered a compelling example of this kind of manipulation when he recalled the way François Mitterand spoke with sym-
pathetic zeal about taking charitable action during the [early years of
the] Yugoslavian disaster, at the time he held the highest office in
France. The former president of the French Republic "remained in
favor, far more than was reasonable, of maintaining Yugoslavia's borders and arguing that only a strong Serbian power would be able to
guarantee some stability in this explosive region."[24] When the news
coverage on television made this position unacceptable to the French
public, Mitterand was forced to make a gesture of some kind. "Humanitarian action and talk permitted [Mitterand] to reaffirm the un-
swerving attachment of France to the rights of man, to mimic opposition to the fascism of Greater Serbia while leaving the way free."[25]
In this case, feeling was the providential ally of cynicism and not, as
one might have expected, its most fearsome enemy.

At the very moment we think we can monitor political actors
under the watchful eye of the television camera, humanitarian man
offers the unanticipated possibility of unloading the terrible burden
of political morality. Abandoning the difficult question of how to do
something, he offers instead a form of narcissistic first aid, distrib-
uted from home, at no personal risk. And he provides this aid in the
name of making the world a more habitable place for those beings,
all the same and all different, who make up humanity.

It was in the name of ideology that we once refused to be taken
in by suffering. It is in opposition to suffering and all the misery in
the world that we now refuse to be taken in by ideology. And so goes
the credulity of the incredulous. Men proceed in the fog, but the
imbeciles show off, as Péguy observed at the dawn of a century that
found its place under the sign of demystification.

six

Of Angels and Men

The Ouménés of Bonnada live next to the Nippos of Pommédé, who are difficult neighbors and not very friendly. To
threaten the Ouménés of Bonnada, the Nibbonis of Bonnaris
join forces with the Nippos of Pommédé or the Rijabons of
Carabule, allying themselves with the Bitules of Rotrarque, or,
by secret agreement after temporarily pacifying them, with the
Rijobettes of Biliguette, who are themselves located on one
side of the Kolvites of Beulet that surround the region belonging to the Ouménés of Bonnada, on the northwest side of the
turitaire, beyond the Prochus of Osteboule, which belongs to
the Nippos of Pommédé.

The situation, of course, does not always look so simple, for
the Ouménés of Bonnada are themselves a cross of four different groups: the Dohommédés of Bonnada, the Odobommédés
of Bonnada, the Orodomédés of Bonnada, and, finally, the
Dovoboddémonédés of Bonnada.[1]

So begins "Le Secret de la situation politique," a satirical poem by
Henri Michaux, who introduces his piece with the epigram "Let us
be clear." Michaux attributes the injunction to Arouet, in other
words, to Voltaire, whose irony comes through the contrast between
the crisp command and the description that follows. Clarity disap-

pears under the weight of all those names, the accumulation without end, the ever more exotic distinctions and divisions, which grow smaller and more refined. It gets lost in the inextricable choreography of war and alliances, in the beat of tom-toms in the bush (the Ouménés of Bonnada) and the hints of headdresses (*bigoudens*) in Brittany (the Rijobettes of Biliguette). The spirit of the Enlightenment grows dark in this great festival of echoing inanities, in which names in capital letters march before us in a never ending procession.

According to Michaux, the secret of our political situation is that it is not political but onomastic. Obtuse identities replace doctrines, principles, and programs. The universal disappears in the singular, the conceptual in the contingent; the beautiful intelligibility of meaning into a totally random muddle. These wars have no stakes to defend, he continues, only labels. Names take the place of divergent opinions and value systems; echoes replace ideology. Whereas some people take these conflicts very seriously, choosing sides between battling signifieds, Michaux finds these situations funny, nothing more than a jumble of indiscernible signifiers. No philosophy arrives in time to give meaning to these arbitrary beings, who are killing themselves in battle, or to offer metaphysical redemption to the shambles made of the idea of history. For Michaux, people who keep looking for reasons to quarrel with one another are worthless, locked up in their stupidities, their collective absurdities. They only exist because they exist, independent of any purpose or reason for being.

In 1991, public opinion in the West saw the world according to Michaux, rising out of the rubble of Communism. Some people used deception in speaking about it, others made jokes, and still others expressed fear, but they all agreed that this soulless new world had become nothing more than groups of people arguing stupidly about borders.

Exhausted by merciless wars, this century is finally coming to an end. After claiming universal solutions with many different ideas, we now celebrate, as we should, the triumph of liberal democracy over its last competitor. But no sooner do we open the first bottles of champagne than squawking nations arise to beat history back. With unpronounceable names, they each take off in their own direction, with their own memories and bizarre chests filled with the past, with flags of long ago, now all fresh and new, exuding a sense of impenetrable artificiality. *Tribalism*: that is the explanation we spontaneously give to this frenetic activity of naming, this unexpected outpouring of heraldry that does not fit the agenda: Slovenia, Slavonia, Slovakia, Croatia, Krajina, Izetbegovic, Milosevic, Karadzic, Silaidzic, Granic, Ganic. We are still falling into the phonetic pit that opened up without warning in this unfortunate region that we once called eastern Europe and conveniently believed was homogenous. "Bosnia-Herzegovina, until very recently, was merely a joke phrase in our language," wrote a columnist for *Newsweek* in 1993, without the slightest trace of embarrassment.[2]

We have seen this before. Fearing more than anything else the possibility of having a gloomy future, we swear not to make the same mistakes again and get taken in by the arguments of one side or the other. But fear alone does not explain why we now prefer bodies to causes. There is another reason as well: today no cause can be universalized. And so after the sickness of history, another disease, more comic but in no way less poisonous, infects men and threatens to turn the world upside down: the sickness of geography. With the end of the cold war, the great confrontation of world systems has been reduced to bitter little wars, to disagreements over borders, to a ridiculous and bloody hotchpotch of squabbles, to the tautology of identity politics. Unable to embrace one side or the other, it makes little sense to defend the identity of either.

This hotchpotch explains, at least in part, why the West remained neutral for so long in our century's last European war. But in addition to its cautious and humanitarian refusal to do anything beyond saving lives, there are positive reasons for not taking a stand: the metaphysical and ethical commitment of Europeans to cosmopolitanism over particularism, to the mixing of races over the absolutism of purity. We thus had to wait for shells to fall on Sarajevo and see its citizens systematically killed, arbitrarily picked off while performing the simple tasks of everyday life, before those who think like Henri Michaux expressed indignation and stopped laughing. Not only did the inhabitants of Sarajevo qualify as victims, but they also lived in the multicultural capital of Bosnia, where cosmopolitanism flourished more visibly than it did in Croatia's city of Vukovar.[3]

Participating in a major conference of writers, scholars, and intellectuals that met in Strasbourg in 1991, between November 8 and 11—two months after the beginning of the siege of Vukovar and ten days before the Yugoslav army entered the city it had destroyed—the sociologist Pierre Bourdieu gave a brief but important talk entitled "The Scientific and Artistic International." In his remarks, he said the following:

> It may be too early, it may be that I am usurping the authority of others, that I have no right to say this here, but I would like us to become a sort of European Parliament of Culture. European, in the sense that this would be a step forward to a higher level of universalization, which for me would already be better than being French.[4]

This "already better" makes Bourdieu, perhaps unwillingly, a direct descendant of Julien Benda, most notably the Benda of *Discours à la nation européene* that the latter wrote in 1932: "Intellectuals of all countries, you must be the ones to tell your nations that they are always in the wrong by the single fact that they are nations. . . . Plotinus blushed at having a body. You should blush at having a nation."[5] As a geographic and material reality, Europe is still cursed by having a body. It is therefore necessary to consider "the European border as only being an illusory permanency in an evolutionary process that does not know how to stop itself."[6] But as Benda explained at the end of his speech, this new body is less carnal than old nations. With Europe, man will have made a great leap forward toward his true destination, even if he remains a prisoner of feeling:

> Because even an impious Europe will necessarily be less impious than the nation. Because it calls for the devotion of man

to a less precise group, less individualized, and consequently less humanly loved, less carnally embraced. The European will inevitably be less attached to Europe than the Frenchman to France or the German to Germany. He will feel much less defined by the soil, less faithful to the land. Even if you make Europe sovereign, the god of immaterialism will smile upon you.[7]

Benda's wish was about to come true at the very moment Bourdieu gave his speech. Still Europe remains the specific determination that separates man from his humanity—hence Bourdieu's reluctance to embrace this identity wholeheartedly. Despite the limitations, by becoming European, the Frenchman transcends the smallness of his native land, expands his plot, and occupies a larger field, one that is more abstract, more rational, and more civilized than the nation—hence Bourdieu's attachment all the same to the European ideal. The intellectual parliament he dreamed about creating opened its doors only two years after the conference in Strasbourg. Sickened by the fighting going on in 1991 and 1992 in the heart of Europe among the Ouménés of Bonnada, the Nippos of Pommédé, and the Nibbonis of Bonnaris, the parliament made Bosnia its cause and announced its intention to do so the first time it met: The god of immaterialism smiled on this country.

In contrast to nations that sinned by the very fact of being nations, Bosnia offered ontological purity and multinational innocence. Emancipated from all lineages, free of all divisions, disagreements, and carnal servitude, its citizens did not have to blush or make excuses about their origins. Their name was more than a name. It was the symbol of cosmopolitanism. Their territory was more than a specific place, it was a scaled-down model of the universal. Being Bosnian was certainly better than being Slovenian, Croatian, Albanian, Macedonian, or Serb.

In 1942, two years after leaving occupied France for the United States and nine years after fleeing Hitler's Germany for France, Hannah

Arendt described the terrible experience of being a refugee, and she did so in the first person plural:

> We lost our home, which means the familiarity of daily life. We lost our occupation, which means the confidence that we are of some use in this world. We lost our language, which means the naturalness of reactions, the simplicity of gestures, the unaffected expression of feelings. We left our relatives in the Polish ghettos and our best friends have been killed in concentration camps, and that means the rupture of our private lives.[8]

Thirty years later, another exile, Jean Améry, continued her description of those who have no community, in an admirable and staggering meditation called "Dans quelle mesure a-t-on besoin d'une terre natale?" In 1939 Jean Améry, whose name at birth was Hans Mayer, lived in Vienna. Because he was Jewish, he had to escape by the smugglers' route and make the long trip to Antwerp at night. Like Arendt, he inherited the same disconcerted "we" deprived of all rights. And under circumstances even more tragic than hers— for he did not escape deportation—Améry met up with the ghostly group of "knights from Without-a-Country, with sad faces, excommunicated"[9] and questioned himself at length about the meaning of nostalgia: "What did this homesickness mean to those banished by the Third Reich for their political opinions or heredity?"[10] To which he responded directly, without beating around the bush, "To long for my country, to long for our country, was alienation from oneself."[11]

In other words, a man feeling homesick does not only long for his country but also for his very identity: "I was a man who could no longer say 'we' and who, for that reason, said 'I' out of habit, without being sustained any more by the feeling of being in full possession of myself."[12] Reduced to himself, the expatriate is no longer himself. Now clearly an orphan, he understands by default that objects—even the most ordinary or functional objects—have meaning beyond their utility. Despite the modern triumph of rational intelligence, "we are still reduced" to live with what makes

us human, "to live among things that tell a story."[13] A world emp-
tied of all symbols, completely subjected to utilitarian thought, is
not truly a world. Under the same painful light of longing, the
refugee sees his mother tongue as not only the language that dom-
inates but also the only language that speaks to him when he
speaks it. By this very fact, it escapes all manipulation. "*Table* will
never be *der Tisch*, anymore than it will necessarily provide enough
to eat."[14]

This infinitesimal but unfathomable difference between two
words that mean the same thing has an impact on even the most
successful exiles, for example, two German immigrants who meet in
New York after having lived there for several years: "Are you happy?" one asks the other. "I am happy," the other answers, *aber glück-
lich bin ich nicht*."[15] I am happy, but happy I am not: the untrans-
latable part of life reveals itself in a joke that resists translation,
leaving Améry to wonder what remained of a life deprived of its
native impenetrability.

The displaced person, said Hannah Arendt, is more representative
than anyone else of the twentieth century. The lesson that this person learns from experience is that man does not gain humanity by
eliminating the past that precedes him, repudiating his origins, and
giving up intuition for an overarching and all-powerful reason. Man
in the abstract, with no people or place, is nothing more than a man.
And as nothing more than a man—as pure consciousness with no
attachments or home—he is no longer a man. What humanizes him
is his particular place in a world endowed with meaning.

As Arendt put it, the "pragmatic force" of the romantic challenge
to the Enlightenment takes on an "irrefutable character"[16] during
the dark times of persecution and exile. If German Jews (or Polish
Jews) saw their native land becoming a nightmare in which deadly
circumstances made them foreigners to their own nostalgia, this second exile in no way canceled out the first. It only made it worse, increasing the torture by refusing these Jews the right to feel any tenderness and shed consoling tears. Because his homeland was hot on
his trail, Améry spent his days pushing away bouts of melancholy

and erasing that part of his life bound up with his lost and predatory country:

> The pain reached its height, to the point of being intolerable,
> when right in the middle of this determined and difficult work
> of self-destruction, good old nostalgia resurfaced, bubbling up
> and demanding its place. The very feelings that social duty and
> desire ordered us to hate rose up suddenly before us, wanting
> to be loved, causing an impossibly neurotic state that no psy-
> choanalytic potion was strong enough to dispel.[17]

Thinking about this unlivable nostalgia well after the attack, Jean
Améry must endure additional trials. He still has to use a password
to prove himself and gain entry into a nervous, vigilant, and suspi-
cious memory. He is not, he insists, "a retard of the *Blut-und-Boden*
army."[18] When he speaks of *Heimat*, he is not dreaming of "Germans of yore, reclining on bearskins."[19] That said, he continues, the
events of this century defy the simplistic conclusion that "the words
soil, country, homeland must be associated with a kind of spiritual
inferiority."[20] Améry has survived the deadly threat of the cult of
belonging, the acts of those who divided humanity and imprisoned
individuals in their race or culture, but he still yearns to belong.

We who read Améry today have recently seen the threat unfold
again in the violent acts of nationalist Serbs in Kosovo, Croatia, and
Bosnia-Herzegovina—as well as in the terrifying acts of the Croatians
in Mostar. Everything suggests that we have not seen the last of this
kind of destructive fanaticism. But as one of the countless pariahs of
this century, uprooted by the madness of those who claim they have
roots, Améry has also had the radical and desperate experience of belonging absolutely nowhere in the world. He is not content, therefore, to turn the state of uprootedness into a positive value or draw
clear distinctions between the sweet air of cosmopolitanism and the
reactionary smells of nostalgia. What he learned from his own deso-
lation is that no particularism had the right to demand the entirety
of his being. But he also learned that he must "have his own land in

order not to need one."[21] It is inhuman, in other words, to define man by blood and soil but no less inhuman to leave him stumbling through life with the terrestrial foundations of his existence taken out from under him. As Améry described it:

> With twenty-seven years of exile behind me, my spiritual com-patriots are Proust, Sartre, Beckett. Yet I am still convinced that the best way to commune with kindred souls of the spirit is to be with fellow countrymen on the streets of a village or in a city. Cultural internationalism can prosper only when one enjoys a secure sense of national belonging.[22]

At the very moment when he must break with his past and cre-ate a new identity, which he does by mixing up the letters of his name, the ex–Hans Mayer makes a major philosophical discovery: all that is given to man and is not constructed, chosen, or desired by him is not necessarily oppressive or alienating. All that conditions his being is not conditioning, for there are limits to the power every-one has over his life, and these limits have the paradoxical virtue of making freedom possible. Like Arendt, Améry is a displaced person, and like her, he is displaced everywhere. He does not, however, con-form to the set of Kantian paradoxes or antinomies that enlightened minds have used to summarize this century. He does not see, in other words, the essence of man as a series of logical steps, follow-ing Lévinas's definition of Hitler's philosophy after 1934[23], or see man as being forcibly separated from this essence. For Améry, man is not, on the one hand, a native attached to his birthplace, nation, and nature or, on the other hand, unattached and free. He refuses to choose between the power of the Other or the autonomy of the ego; the feeling of gratitude toward what is given or the capacity to think, feel, and act by oneself; the weight of being or the lightness of being; genealogical inscription or individual affirmation; identity or humanity. No matter what form it takes, this dualism violently distorts our understanding of the human condition. Recognizing that this kind of thinking was inadequate, Hannah Arendt and Jean

Améry spent the rest of their lives trying to paste the two parts back together again.

104 This impossible postwar. With the fall of Communism, the last of the two great systems, the revolutionary illusion is dead, but not the disjunctive approach to reality on which this illusion was built. The victory of Democracy did not destroy the great dualism that the Communist idea had used for so many years and with such success. In fact, quite the opposite has occurred, as we see by the ongoing spirit of Julien Benda through the work of Pierre Bourdieu. The great novelist Mario Vargas Llosa demonstrated this explicitly as well when he proclaimed:

> One of the ideals of our youth is being realized today—the disappearance of borders, the integration of the world's countries into a single system of exchange that benefits everyone, especially those who urgently need to leave underdevelopment behind. But contrary to what we believed would happen, it was not the socialist revolution that made this world one, but its archenemies: capitalism and the market. Still, this is the most beautiful advance in modern history because it lays the foundations for a new civilization on a global scale that organizes itself around political democracy, civil society, economic freedom, and the rights of man.[24]

Nothing could be clearer: liberal democracy replaces its successor with its market economy, free elections, and the rights of man. Society is independent of power, and man is finally human because he is finally universal. To complete the inventory of this apotheosis, we must add the fourth component to the new world civilization, identified and celebrated by Vargas Llosa, namely, technology, or more precisely, information technology. To quote Nicholas Negroponte, the director of MIT's Media Lab, "Computing is not about computers any more. It is about living."[25] Each object, product, book, painting, museum, and monument has its digital equivalent. Now that everyone is equipped (or is on the point of being equipped) with a screen, and these screens are connected to the worldwide web, no place, no matter how far away, is beyond the reach of a portable machine, be it on land, in the air, or on sea. From now on, everybody can be contacted, and everything passed on with a simple command; just a click will do.

As our century draws to a close, we would not have honored this technology by calling it a *revolution* if it were only a more efficient prosthesis or piece of equipment. It is much more than that. The services offered by the total screen have radically changed our relationship to reality. From now on, man has a place, but the place has no claim on him. His location is no longer tied to a special address. Once he believed he was doomed to the here and now, dominated by real time. Now everything is now, and the word *here* means virtually nothing. In the age of electronic mail, an address—the humble and obligatory response to the question "where?"—is no longer a place, it is movable. "Most American children do not know the difference between the Baltics and the Balkans, or who the Visigoths were, or when Louis XIV lived. So what? Why are those so important? Did you know that Reno is west of Los Angeles?"[26]

Indeed, why be shocked? Now that technology has replaced topology, the human experience—all too human—of living side by side is giving way to the Olympian drunkenness of a universal equidistance. Man is no longer indigenous, native to one place; he is global. His immediate environment is no longer local but digital. Once tied to a territory and people, now he is plugged into a network and can make his own virtual community. Belonging to the world was his destiny; now summoning the world gives him freedom. Cybernetic and proud, he can let go of the obscene materiality of things for the unending pleasures of insubstantial space. Once geographical and historical, he is now angelic, shielded like the angels from the exhaustion of life and the demands of the body, able to enjoy the gift of ubiquity and weightlessness. Before he was accountable to the memory of much earlier times that made demands and insisted on his specificity. Now he is free, with no burden of a past. He is no longer invaded by the already there, by this intimate otherness, this prejudicial wound inflicted on the dream of autarky, by this inner presence of the dead called ironically, no doubt, identity.

106   This is the end of inclusive identities. Widespread communication and connection have performed a miraculous job of plastic surgery, erasing the lines of geographic borders that had previously been sculpted into the face of humanity. Ties imposed on us have given way to relationships freely chosen, even among the dead. What happiness awaits us! People can give their child a name from any place on earth, plug themselves in without leaving their room to any entertainment they want, watch catastrophes as they unfold on the screen, explore far-off cultures slumped down in a chair, arrive unannounced down memory lane, go window-shopping in bedroom slippers on the other side of the globe, wander about at will in a jumble of cultures, gathered up in a great data bank that serves as the depository of the world's many traditions. One used to be in one place or another, inside or out, at home or abroad, bourgeois or unconventional, a homebody or a wanderer. The age of "either-or" is finished, and a new period has begun in which the tourist replaces the inhabitant. Thus with the elimination of distances and destinies, we have entered a new era in which everyone becomes a visitor to everything.

As Chateaubriand wondered:

What would a universal society be like without individual countries? Where there would be no French, no English, no German, no Spanish, no Portuguese, no Russian, no Tartan, no Turkish, no Persian, no Italian, no Chinese, no American, or, rather, where all these societies would be one? What would its understanding of the world look like, its customs, science, art, and poetry? Thanks to the speed of travel, would you have lunch in Paris and supper in Peking? How wonderful, but then what? How would the passions felt by peoples living in different places be expressed at the same time? How would this confusion of needs and images enter into the language? How

would the products of different suns nourish a single conception of youth, manhood, and old age? And in what language
would they be communicated?[27]

Society today is nourished by the one and eternal sun of multi-
media. Technology in our time has made Chateaubriand's anxious
fantasy come true. And in our new world, morality has embraced
this new reality as the realization of the ideal.

For global man, violence comes from a sense of belonging; ethnic
cleansing is the direct and natural response to an impure desire to
hold on to a particular reality. In the eyes of global man who loves
the immaterial, heaviness is at the origin of all horrors. For this trav-
eler who does not move, war dates from an earlier time, developing
out of a preangelic opposition between the here and the elsewhere.
Evil, in other words, comes to the world through fatherlands and
patronyms. Evil is the dead taking hold of the living, the dictatorship of family names over first names. Evil is the spirit that does not
fly away. It crashes down instead and becomes flesh. Evil is incarnation. How stupid the earth is! And what a relief to see a new rebel-
lious generation emerge on the inspired hills and virtual countryside
of the cherubic screen! How comfortable this fluid and light universe
is, smooth and undulating, dancing and ductile, in which nothing
expires or escapes forever, in which everything is frequented, ex-
changed, mixed, and combined at will, where everyone, in a word,
is finally free to claim: "I am the world and the world is me!"[28]

"Modern man trades in his land for the world. A pretty good deal,"[29]
exclaimed Jean Améry, who was not far from thinking as Chesterton
did that "the globe-trotter lives in a smaller world than the peas-
ant."[30] But he did not know that this pretty good deal would be cut
on his back and in his name. The experience of displaced persons has
led modern man to conclude that the desire to have roots was the
modern sin of the flesh. Nor did Améry expect modern man to summarize what he learned from the twentieth century as a dizzying
choice between tourism and barbarism.

Here, for example, is what Pierre Nora, the author of the masterful *Lieux de mémoires* (*Realms of Memory*), wrote about this monumental inventory of places and symbols that determined French identity:

> Measured by traditional criteria, feelings of national pride may seem to be diminishing. But these feelings have probably changed less in intensity than in scale or style of expression. . . . Once aggressive and military, they now are competitive, entirely invested in the cult of industrial performance and sports. Instead of sacrifice and death, they now focus on pleasure, curiosity, and, one might say, tourism. Instead of seeking to teach, they are obsessed with the media; instead of thinking collectively, they look out for the individual, becoming even individualistic. France *à la carte*, France *carte-menu*, France *carte Michelin*.[31]

Read about Michelet in *Michelin*; substitute the aesthetic or gastronomic paradigm for the model of sacrifice; cancel all debts to the dead in exchange for an accessible past; turn patriotic duty into patrimonial pleasure, commitment into ritual tasting. Transform the citizen into observer; dissolve time into space, the normative into the recreational, the political into the cultural. Take a grand tour, touching base in lavish style with the ties of long ago, with all the old controversies. The consumer removes the bellicose nationalist from combat while the nation enters into a new age of self-service. In sum, modern man can be proud of the progress he has made. Tourist of himself and tourist of the other, he visits the world as he would an immense amusement park, an interminable museum in which both identity and difference offer themselves up for observation at his discretion.

Tourism, in other words, is not simply the itinerant way that sedentary moderns fill their free time, it is the state toward which humanity is heading. As the world takes stock of itself, this state of tourism is highly valued. It accedes, moreover, to the rank of the sovereign good. "All tourists, tourists forever!" That is the final expression of emancipation and brotherhood. What claims today the beautiful name of cosmopolitanism is no longer, to cite Hannah Arendt once again, "a readiness to share the world with other men"[32] but a globalization of me. It is no longer this broadened attitude of mind, admirably defined by Kant as the ability of thought to imagine other points of view, but an expansion of subjectivity and of the inherent quality of global man finally getting out of a state of limbo.

Nietzsche used to say, "The desert is growing bigger. Woe unto him who protects the desert!" And woe unto us, for as Chateaubriand worried and Nietzsche predicted, globalization is gaining, and the desert is expanding. Despite Améry's teachings, it is the memory of disaster that protects this desert as if our century had only taken place to ban nostalgia from the land and make sure that all operations were in good working order.

Epilogue

IN THE FINAL PAGES of the first edition of *The Origins of Totalitarianism,* which was published in England under the title of *The Burden of Our Time,* Hannah Arendt used the word *resentment*[1] to characterize the predominant mood of modern man. Resentment against "everything given, even his own existence," resentment against "the very fact that he is not the creator of the universe and himself." Driven by this fundamental resentment, modern man is unable to "see rhyme or reason in the given world." Instead he "proclaims openly that everything is permitted and believes secretly that everything is possible."[2]

Everything is possible: this axiom revealed its devastating power in the crimes committed for universal humanism and for justifying the idea of a superior humanity. Drawing lessons from the catastrophe, Hannah Arendt went on to claim that the only alternative to the nihilism of resentment is gratitude:

> a fundamental gratitude for the few elementary things that indeed are invariably given us, such as life itself, the existence of man and the world. . . . In the sphere of politics, gratitude emphasizes that we are not alone in the world. We can reconcile ourselves to the variety of mankind, to the differences between human beings . . . only through insight into the tremendous

bliss that man was created with the power of procreation, that not a single man but Men inhabit the earth.[3]

112 Have we reconciled ourselves? In the name of diversity, worldwide webs are building a global society. Angelic, busy, and vigilant, their apostles believe they embody resistance to all acts of inhumanity. But to exchange old demons for new networks of communication is to make a mistake. Beneath the edifying appearance of a primordial combat, information technology obscures the fact that friendship has disappeared into sentimentality, and mass tourism has erased traditional distinctions between near and far. This, in the end, is the worldwide victory of those who have succeeded in bringing together the same with the same over those seeking to build a common world with a shared idea of humanity, based on gratitude.

Life goes on, things happen, but nothing seems exciting enough to change modern man. Feelings reign freely, and ideology is defeated—at least for the time being—but the new age has not conquered the empire of resentment. Has the twentieth century therefore been useless?

notes

The Last of the Just

1. Primo Levi, *Survival at Auschwitz*, trans. Stuart Woolf (New York: Collier, 1993), pp. 105–6.

2. William Shakespeare, *The Merchant of Venice* (Cambridge: Cambridge University Press, 1926), p. 43.

3. Emmanuel Lévinas, *Difficult Freedom: Essays on Judaism*, trans. Sean Hand (Baltimore: Johns Hopkins University Press, 1990), pp. 152–53; (in French) *Difficile liberté* (Paris: Albin Michel, 1976), p. 201.

4. Ibid., p. 153; French, p. 202.

chapter one Who Is Like Unto Me?

1. Claude Lévi-Strauss, *Structural Anthropology*, vol. 2, trans. Monique Layton (Chicago: University of Chicago Press, 1983), p. 329; (in French) *Anthropologie structurale, deux* (Paris: Plon, 1973), pp. 383–84.

2. Lev. 24:22, *The Jerusalem Bible* (Garden City, N.Y.: Doubleday, 1966), p. 134.

3. Emmanuel Lévinas, *Difficult Freedom: Essays on Judaism*, trans. Sean Hand (Baltimore: Johns Hopkins University Press, 1990), p. 178; (in French) *Difficile liberté* (Paris: Albin Michel, 1976), p. 232.

4. Rémi Brague, "Cosmos et éthique: La Fin d'un modèle," *Acta institutionis philosophiae et aestheticae* 12 (1994): 56–57.

5. Plato, *Timaeus*, ed. and trans. with an introduction by John Warrington (New York: Dutton, 1965); (in French) *Timée* (Paris: GF-Flammarion, 1982), p. 144.

6. Aristotle, *The Politics of Aristotle*, trans. Ernest Baker (Oxford: Oxford University Press, 1946), p. 13; (in French) *Politique* (Paris: Vrin, 1982), pp. 40–41.

7. Gal. 3:28, *The Jerusalem Bible*, p. 243.

8. Cited by Georges Duby in *The Three Orders: Feudal Society Imagined*, trans. Arthur Goldhammer (Chicago: University of Chicago Press, 1978), p. 3; (in French) *Les Trois Ordres ou l'imaginaire du féodalisme* (Paris: Gallimard, 1978), pp. 89–90.

9. Alexis de Tocqueville, *Democracy in America*, vol. 2, trans. Henry Reeve, rev. Francis Bowen (Mattituck, N.Y.: Amereon House, 1993), pp. 166; (in French) *De la démocratie en Amérique* (Paris: Robert Laffont, coll. "Bouquins," 1986), p. 542.

10. Ibid., p. 163; French, p. 540.

11. Bartolomé de las Casas, *The Devastation of the Indies*, trans. Herma Briffault, with an introduction by Bill M. Donovan (Baltimore: Johns Hopkins University Press, 1992), p. 8.

12. Cited in Mariane Mahn-Lot, *Bartolomé de las Casas et le droit des Indiens* (Paris: Payot, 1995), p. 168.

13. Cited by Tzvetan Todorov, *The Conquest of America: The Question of the Other*, trans. Richard Howard (New York: Harper & Row, 1984), p. 152; (in French) *La Conquête de l'Amérique* (Paris: Editions du Seuil, 1982), p. 158.

14. Cited by Lewis Hanke, *The Spanish Struggle for Justice in the Conquest of America* (Philadelphia: University of Pennsylvania Press, 1949), p. 122.

15. Las Casas, cited by Alain Milhou, preface to *La Destruction des Indes de Bartolomé de las Casas* (Paris: Chandeigne, 1995), p. 49.

16. See Ernst Cassirer, *The Individual and the Cosmos in Renaissance Philosophy*, trans. with an introduction by Mario Domand (New York: Harper & Row, 1964), pp. 7–45.

17. Cited by Mahn-Lot, *Bartolomé de las Casas*, p. 170.

18. Cited by Hanke, *The Spanish Struggle for Justice*, p. 128.

19. Cited by Mariane Mahn-Lot, "Las Casas et les cultures païennes," *Le Supplément, Revue d'éthique* (June 1995).

20. Michel Montaigne, *Essays and Selected Writings: A Bilingual Edition*, trans. and ed. Donald M. Frame (New York: St. Martin's Press, 1963), p. 89; (in French) *Essais* (Paris: Gallimard, coll. "Bibliothèque pléiade," 1962), p. 203.

21. Montesquieu, *The Spirit of the Laws*, vol. 1, trans. Thomas Nugent (New York: Colonial Press, 1899), p. 138; (in French) *De l'esprit des lois*, vol. 1 (Paris: Gallimard, coll. "Folio essais," 1995), p. 472.

22. Lévi-Strauss, *Structural Anthropology*, vol. 2, p. 330; French, p. 384.

23. Blaise Pascal, *Pascal's Pensées*, trans. with an introduction by H. F. Stewart (New York: Pantheon, 1950), p. 41; (in French) *Pensées*, ed. Léon Brunschvicg (Paris: Le Livre de poche, 1972), p. 42.

24. Ibid., p. 43, French, p. 44.

25. Blaise Pascal, *Thoughts, Letters and Minor Works*, vol. 48, *Minor Works*, **115** trans. W. F. Trotter, M. L. Booth, and O. W. Wight (New York: Collier & Son, 1910), p. 384; "Trois discours sur la condition des grands," in Blaise Pascal, *Pensées sur la politique* (Paris: Rivages-Poche, 1992), pp. 108–9.

26. Tocqueville, *Democracy in America*, p. 181; French, p. 552.

27. Cited by Paul Vernière, *Lumières ou clair-obscur* (Paris: PUF, 1987), p. 196.

28. I borrow this expression from Robert Legros, "La Reconnaissance sensible de l'homme par l'homme," EPOKHE 2, Jérôme Millon, 1991, pp. 236–62. See also Robert Legros, *L'Idée d'humanité: Introduction à la phénoménologie* (Paris: Grasset, 1990), a magnificent book that has greatly influenced the ideas presented in this chapter.

29. Tocqueville, *Democracy in America*, p. 165; French, p. 541.

30. Emilio Lussu, *Sardinian Brigade*, trans. Marion Rawson (New York: Knopf, 1939), pp. 166–67.

31. Ibid., pp. 169–70.

32. Vladimir Jankélévitch, *Traité des vertus: Les Vertus et l'amour*, vol. 2 (Paris: Bordas, 1970), p. 1016.

chapter two The Glamorous Appeal of the Common Noun

1. Raymond Aron, *The Committed Observer: Interviews with Jean-Louis Missika and Dominique Wolton*, trans. James and Marie McIntosh (Chicago: Regnery Gateway, 1983), p. 95; (in French) *Le Spectateur engagé: Entretiens avec Jean-Louis Missika et Dominique Wolton* (Paris: Presses-Pocket, 1983), p. 115.

2. Jean-Paul Sartre, *Anti-Semite and Jew*, trans. George J. Becker (New York: Schocken Books, 1948), pp. 22–23, 27 (italics in original); (in French) *Réflexions sur la question juive* (Paris: Gallimard, coll. "Folio essais," 1985), pp. 25–26, 30–31.

3. Ibid., pp. 53–54; French, pp. 62–63.

4. Michel Foucault, *Dits et écrits* (Paris: Gallimard, coll. "Bibliothèque des sciences humaines," 1994), vol. 4, p. 686.

5. Jean-Paul Sartre, *Existentialism and Humanism*, trans. with an introduction by Philip Mairet (London: Methuen, 1946), p. 26; (in French) *L'Existentialisme est un humanisme* (Paris: Nagel, 1970), p. 18.

6. Ibid., p. 28; French, pp. 21–22.

7. Pic de La Mirandole, *Oeuvres philosophiques* (Paris: PUF, 1993), pp. 5–7.

8. Jean-Paul Sartre, *Being and Nothingness*, trans. Hazel Barnes (New York: Philosophical Library, 1956), p. 59; (in French) *L'Etre et le néant* (Paris: Gallimard, 1943), pp. 98–99.

9. Ibid., p. 528; French, p. 637.

10. Witold Gombrowicz, *Diary*, vol. 2 (1957–61), trans. Lillian Vallee (Evanston, Ill.: Northwestern University Press, 1989), p. 5.

11. Jean-Paul Sartre, foreword to André Gorz, *The Traitor*, trans. Richard Howard (London: Verso, 1989), p. 14; (in French) préface par Sartre au *Traître* (Paris: Editions du Seuil, 1958), p. 26.

12. Sartre, *Existentialism and Humanism*, p. 52; French, pp. 84–85.

13. Sartre, *Anti-Semite and Jew*, p. 54; French, pp. 63–64.

14. Emmanuel Lévinas, *Difficult Freedom: Essays on Judaism*, trans. Sean Hand (Baltimore: Johns Hopkins University Press, 1990) (passage not translated in English); (in French) *Difficile liberté* (Paris: Albin Michel, 1976), p. 374.

15. Emmanuel Lévinas, *Altérité et transcendance* (Montpellier: Fata Morgana, 1995), p. 134.

16. Lévinas, *Difficile liberté*, p. 24.

17. Emmanuel Lévinas, *Humanisme de l'autre homme* (Montpellier: Fata Morgana, 1972), p. 15.

18. Emmanuel Lévinas, *Beyond the Verse: Talmudic Readings and Lectures*, trans. Gary D. Mole (Bloomington: Indiana University Press, 1994), p. 190; (in French) *L'Au-delà du verset* (Paris: Editions du Minuit, 1982), p. 223.

19. Emmanuel Lévinas, *Otherwise Than Being or Beyond Essence*, trans. Alphonso Lingis (Dorderecht: Kluwer Academic Publishers, 1991), p. 88; (in French) *Autrement qu'être ou au-delà de l'essence* (The Hague: Nijhoff, 1978), p. III.

20. Paul Ricoeur, *Réflexion faite: Autobiographie intellectuelle* (Paris: Editions Esprit, 1995), p. 33.

21. Roland Barthes, *The Rustle of Language*, trans. Richard Howard (New York: Hill & Wang, 1986), p. 31; (in French) *Le Bruissement de la langue: Essais critiques*, vol. 4 (Paris: Editions du Seuil, 1984), p. 35.

22. Aimé Césaire, *Discourse on Colonialism*, trans. Joan Pinkham (New York: Monthly Review Press, 1972), p. 14; (in French) *Discours sur le colonialisme* (Paris: Présence africaine, 1989), p. 12.

23. Karl Marx, *The German Ideology, Part 1*, trans. R. Ryazanskaya, in *The Marx-Engels Reader*, 2nd ed., ed. Robert C. Tucker (New York: Norton, 1978), p. 170 (italics in original).

24. Jean-Paul Sartre, preface to Frantz Fanon's *The Wretched of the Earth*, trans. Constance Farrington (New York: Grove Weidenfeld, 1963), pp. 24–25; (in French) *Les Damnés de la terre* (Paris: Gallimard, coll. "Folio Actuel," 1991), p. 55.

25. Jacques Derrida, *Moscou aller-retour* (Paris: Editions de l'Aube, 1995), p. 17–18.

26. Roland Barthes, *Oeuvres complètes*, vol. 1 (Paris: Editions du Seuil, 1993), p. 755 (italics in original).

27. Claude Lefort, *Les Formes de l'histoire: Essais d'anthropologie politique* (Paris: Gallimard, 1978), p. 254.

28. Michel Foucault, "What Is Enlightenment?" in *The Foucault Reader*, trans. and ed. Paul Rabinow (New York: Pantheon Books, 1984), p. 50; (in French) "Qu'est-ce que les lumières?" in Foucault, *Dits et écrits*, vol. 4, p. 578.

29. Foucault, *Dits et écrits*, vol. 4, p. 167.

30. Michel Foucault, "Truth, Power, Self: An Interview with Michel Foucault," with Rux Martin, in *Technologies of the Self: A Seminar with Michel Foucault*, ed. L. Martin, H. Gutman, and P. Hutton (Amherst: University of Massachusetts Press, 1988), p. 10; Foucault, *Dits et écrits*, vol. 4, p. 778.

31. Michel Foucault, *Power/Knowledge: Selected Interviews and Other Writings*, 1972–1977, ed. Colin Gordon, trans. Colin Gordon et al. (New York: Pantheon Press, 1980), p. 80; *Dits et écrits*, vol. 3 (Paris: Gallimard, 1994), p. 163.

32. Ibid.

33. Foucault, "What Is Enlightenment?" p. 46; French, p. 574.

34. Sartre, *Being and Nothingness*, p. 35; French, p. 72.

chapter three The Triumph of the Will

1. Julien Benda, *The Treason of the Intellectuals*, trans. R. Aldington (New York: Norton, 1969), p. 79; (in French) *La Trahison des clercs* (Paris: Jean-Jacques Pauvert, 1965), p. 68.

2. Ibid., p. 95; French, p. 81.

3. Julien Benda, *La Fin de l'éternel* (Paris: Gallimard, 1977), p. 43 (italics in original).

4. Louis Althusser, *Lenin and Philosophy and Other Essays*, trans. Ben Brewster (London: NLB, 1971), p. 7; (in French) *Lénine et la philosophie* (Paris: Maspéro, 1972), p. 7.

5. Julien Benda, quoted by Louis-Albert Revah, *Julien Benda* (Paris: Plon, 1991), p. 253.

6. Hannah Arendt, *The Origins of Totalitarianism*, New Ed. (New York: Harcourt Brace & World, 1966), p. viii (italics in original).

7. François Furet, *Le Passé d'une illusion: Essai sur l'idée communiste au XXe siècle* (Paris: Robert Laffont / Calmann-Lévy, 1995), p. 496 (italics in original).

8. Adolf Hitler, cited in Norman Cohn, *Warrant for Genocide: The Myth of the Jewish World-Conspiracy and the Protocols of the Elders of Zion* (New York: Harper & Row, 1967), p. 182.

9. Adam Müller, cited by Albert O. Hirschman, *The Rhetoric of Reaction:*

Perversity, Futility, Jeopardy (Cambridge, Mass.: Harvard University Press, 1991),
118 p. 14.

10. Joseph de Maistre, *Les Soirées de Saint-Pétersbourg*, vol. 2, ed. Guy Trédaniel (Paris: Editions de la Maisnie, 1991), p. 82.

11. Odo Marquard, "Questions à la philosophie de l'histoire," in *Situations de la démocratie*, ed. La Pensée politique (Paris: Hautes études/Gallimard/Le Seuil, 1993), p. 215.

12. Hermann Rauschning, *The Voice of Destruction* (New York: Putnam, 1940), p. 238.

13. Edmund Burke, *Reflections on the Revolution in France*, ed. with an introduction by J. G. A. Pocock (Indianapolis: Hackett, 1987), p. 195.

14. Adolf Hitler, *Mein Kampf*, cited in Philippe Burrin, *Hitler and the Jews: The Genesis of the Holocaust*, trans. Patsy Southgate with an introduction by Saul Friedlander (London: Arnold, 1994), p. 30; (in French) *Hitler et les Juifs: Genèse d'un génocide* (Paris: Editions du Seuil, 1989), p. 25.

15. Arendt, *The Origins of Totalitarianism*, p. 463.

16. Alexis de Tocqueville, *The European Revolution & Correspondence with Gobineau*, ed., trans., and with an introduction by John Lukacs (Westport, Conn.: Greenwood Press, 1959), p. 224; (in French) *Correspondance Tocqueville-Gobineau*, in *Oeuvres complètes*, vol. 9 (Paris: Gallimard, 1960), p. 199.

17. Ibid., pp. 231–32; French, p. 203.

18. Adolf Hitler, quoted by Rauschning, *The Voice of Destruction*, p. 232.

19. Hannah Arendt, *Eichmann in Jerusalem* (New York: Penguin Books, 1994), p. 150.

20. Charles Péguy, *Note conjointe sur Monsieur Descartes . . .* , in *Oeuvres en prose complètes*, vol. 3 (Paris: Gallimard, coll. "Bibliothèque de la pléiade," 1992), p. 1443.

21. Ibid., p. 1444.

22. Heinrich Himmler, *Discours secrets* (Paris: Gallimard, coll. "Folio histoire," 1978), p. 167.

23. Ibid., p. 168.

24. Hitler, *Mein Kampf*, cited by Eberhard Jäckel, *Hitler idéologue* (Paris: Gallimard, 1995), p. 72.

25. Himmler, *Discours secrets*, p. 206.

26. Ian Kershaw, "Retour sous le totalitarisme," *Esprit* (January–February 1996): 115–16. The article was reprinted from an issue of the *Tel-Aviv Jahrbuch für Deutsche Geschichte*.

27. Gilbert K. Chesterton, *Orthodoxy* (New York: Dodd, Mead, 1945), p. 61.

28. Arthur Koestler, *Darkness at Noon*, trans. Daphne Hardy (New York: Bantam Books, 1968), p. 153 (italics added).

29. Ibid., pp. 137, 141.

30. Claude Lévi-Strauss, *Structural Anthropology*, vol. 2, trans. Monique Layton (Chicago: University of Chicago Press, 1983), p. 40; (in French) *Anthropologie structurale*, deux (Paris: Plon, 1973), p. 52.

31. Ibid. (italics in original).

32. Milan Kundera, *The Unbearable Lightness of Being*, trans. Michael H. Heim (New York: Harper Perennial, 1991) p. 289.

33. Hannah Arendt, *Lectures on Kant's Political Philosophy*, ed. with an interpretive essay by Ronald Beiner (Chicago: University of Chicago Press, 1982), p. 77.

34. Ernst Renan, *L'Avenir de la science*, in *Oeuvres complètes*, vol. 3 (Paris: Calmann-Lévy, 1949), p. 1030.

35. Ibid., pp. 883–84.

36. Arendt, *Lectures on Kant's Political Philosophy*, p. 77.

37. Arendt, *The Origins of Totalitarianism*, pp. 470–71.

38. Ibid., p. 471.

39. Roland Barthes, *Oeuvres complètes*, vol. 1 (Paris: Editions du Seuil, 1993), p. 106.

chapter four The Irony of History

1. François Furet, *Le Passé d'une illusion: Essai sur l'idée communiste au XXe siècle* (Paris: Robert Laffont / Calmann-Lévy, 1995), p. 45.

2. Charles Péguy, *Note conjointe sur Monsieur Descartes* . . . , in *Oeuvres en prose complètes*, vol. 3 (Paris: Gallimard, coll. "Bibliothèque de la Pléiade," 1992), pp. 1343–44.

3. Sebastian Haffner, *The Ailing Empire: Germany from Bismarck to Hitler*, trans. Jean Steinberg (New York: Fromm International, 1991), pp. 95–96; (in French) *De Bismarck à Hitler, une histoire du Reich allemand* (Paris: La Découverte, 1991), p. 74.

4. Raymond Aron, *Les Guerres en chaîne* (Paris: Gallimard, 1951), p. 30.

5. Homer, *The Iliad*, trans. Richmond Lattimore (Chicago: University of Chicago Press, 1951), p. 443.

6. Ernst Jünger, *Le Travailleur* (Paris: Christian Bourgeois, 1989), pp. 194–95; (in German) *Der Arbeiter: Herrschaft und Gestalt* (Hamburg: Hanseatische Verlagsanstalt, 1932).

7. Dominique Janicaud, *Powers of the Rational: Science, Technology and the Future of Thought*, trans. Peg Birmingham and Elizabeth Birmingham (Bloomington: Indiana University Press, 1994), p. 31; (in French) *La Puissance du rationnel* (Paris: Gallimard, 1985), p. 52.

8. Joseph Roth, *The Radetzky March*, trans. Eva Tucker (New York: Overlook Press, 1974), p. 107.

9. Ernst Renan, *L'Avenir de la science*, in *Oeuvres complètes*, vol. 3 (Paris: **120** Calmann-Lévy, 1949), p. 883.

10. Franz Rosenzweig, *The Star of Redemption*, trans. William W. Hallo (New York: Holt, Rinehart and Winston, 1970), p. 3.

11. Franz Rosenzweig, cited by Stéphane Mosès, *Système et révélation: La Philosophie de Franz Rosenzweig* (Paris: Editions du Seuil, 1982), p. 34.

12. Paul Valéry, "The Crisis of the Mind," in *The Collected Works of Paul Valéry*, vol. 10, *History and Politics*, Bollingen Series 45, no. 10, trans. Denise Folliot and Jackson Matthews, with a preface by François Valéry and an introduction by Salvador de Madriaga (New York: Bollingen/Pantheon, 1962), p. 23; (in French) "La Crise de l'esprit," in *Variété* 1 et 2 (Paris: Gallimard, coll. "Idées," 1978), p. 15.

13. Renan, *L'Avenir de la science*, p. 1011.

14. Valéry, "The Crisis of the Mind," p. 24; French, p. 15 (italics in original).

15. Hannah Arendt, *The Origins of Totalitarianism*, New Ed. (New York: Harcourt Brace & World, 1966), p. 267.

16. Furet, *Le Passé d'une illusion*, p. 115.

17. Vladimir Lenin, cited by Dominique Colas, *Le Léninisme* (Paris: PUF, 1982), p. 66.

18. Carl von Clausewitz, *On War*, trans. Michael Howard and Peter Paret (Princeton, N.J.: Princeton University Press, 1976), p. 87.

19. Raymond Aron, *Peace and War: A Theory of International Relations*, trans. Richard Howard and Annette Baker Fox (New York: Doubleday, 1966), p. 26; (in French) *Paix et guerre entre les nations* (Paris: Calmann-Lévy, 1984), p. 38.

20. Clausewitz, *On War*, p. 87.

21. Lenin, cited in Colas, *Le Léninisme*, p. 64.

22. Ibid., p. 101.

23. Cited by Norman Cohn, *Warrant for Genocide: The Myth of the Jewish World-Conspiracy and the Protocols of the Elders of Zion* (New York: Harper & Row, 1967), p. 136.

24. Jünger, *Le Travailleur*, p. 209. See also Jeffrey Herf, *Reactionary Modernism: Technology, Culture, and Politics in Weimar and the Third Reich* (Cambridge: Cambridge University Press, 1984).

25. George Orwell, *The Collected Essays, Journalism and Letters*, vol. 2, ed. Sonia Orwell and Ian Angus (New York: Harcourt Brace & World, 1968), p. 142.

26. Ibid., pp. 143–44.

27. Ibid., p. 142.

28. Ibid., p. 143.

29. Ibid.

30. Arendt, *The Origins of Totalitarianism*, p. 457 (italics added).

31. Ibid., p. 455.

32. Primo Levi, *Survival in Auschwitz*, trans. Stuart Woolf (New York: Collier, 1993), p. 90.

33. Varlam Shalamov, *Kolyma Tales*, trans. John Glad (New York: Norton, 1980) (passage not translated in English ed.); (in French) *Kolyma: Récits de la vie des camps*, vol. 1 (Paris: Maspéro, 1980), p. 19.

34. Alexander Solzhenitsyn, "The Nobel Prize Lecture on Literature," trans. Alexis Klimoff, in his *East and West* (New York: Harper & Row Perennial, 1980), pp. 18–19.

35. Primo Levi, *The Reawakening*, trans. Stuart Woolf (New York: Collier, 1965), p. 11.

36. Ibid., p. 12.

37. Jules Michelet, *Histoire de France: Le Moyen Age*, (Paris: Robert Laffont, coll. "Bouquins," 1981), p. 629.

chapter five Humanitarian Amends

1. Milan Kundera, *The Art of the Novel*, trans. Linda Asher (New York: Grove Press, 1986), p. 141; (in French) *L'Art du roman* (Paris: Gallimard, 1986), p. 172.

2. Aleksander Wat, *My Century: The Odyssey of a Polish Intellectual*, trans. Richard Lourie (Berkeley and Los Angeles: University of California Press, 1988), p. 69.

3. Ibid., p. 22.

4. Ibid., p. 86.

5. Henri Dunant, *A Memory of Solferino*, trans. by the volunteers of the Red Cross's District of Columbia chapter (Geneva: International Committee of the Red Cross, 1986), p. 44; (in French) *Un souvenir de Solferino* (Paris: L'Age d'homme, 1986), pp. 31–32.

6. Jean-Jacques Rousseau, *Emile: Or on Education*, trans. with an introduction by Allan Bloom (New York: Basic Books, 1979), p. 162; (in French) *Emile ou de l'éducation* (Paris: Garnier, 1961), p. 260.

7. Dunant, *A Memory* (passage not translated in English ed.); French, p. 120.

8. See Alain Destexhe, *L'Humanitaire impossible ou deux siècles d'ambiguïté* (Paris: Armand Colin, 1993).

9. Jean Christophe Rufin, *Le Piège humanitaire* (Paris: Hachette, coll. "Pluriel," 1993), p. 62.

10. See Trotsky, in Leon Trotsky, John Dewey, and George Novack, *Their Morals and Ours: Marxist Versus Liberal Views on Morality* (New York: Merit Publishers, 1969).

11. Emmanuel Lévinas, "La Souffrance inutile," in *Entre nous: Essais sur le penser-à-l'autre* (Paris: Grasset, 1991), p. 116.

12. Jean-Jacques Rousseau, *The Social Contract and Discourses*, trans. G. D. H. Cole (London: Dent, Everyman's Library, 1973), p. 75; (in French) *Discours sur l'origine et les fondements de l'inégalité parmi les hommes* (Paris: Flammarion, 1971), p. 198.

13. Ibid.

14. Michel Foucault, *Dits et écrits* (Paris: Gallimard, coll. "Bibliothèque des sciences humaines," 1994), vol. 4, p. 708.

15. Michel Serres, *Angels, a Modern Myth*, trans. Francis Cowper, ed. Philippa Hurd (Paris: Flammarion, 1995); (in French) *La Légende des anges* (Paris: Flammarion, 1993), p. 249.

16. Johann Wolfgang Goethe, *Selections from Goethe's Letters to Frau von Stein, 1776–1789*, ed. and trans. Robert M. Browning (Columbia, N.C.: Camden House, 1990), p. 294.

17. Georges Bernanos, *Nous autres Français* (Paris: Editions du Seuil, coll. "Points essais," 1984), p. 205.

18. Régis Debray, *L'Oeil naïf* (Paris: Editions du Seuil, 1985), pp. 155.

19. Ibid., p. 156.

20. Paul Ricoeur, *Time and Narrative*, vol. 3, trans. Kathleen Balamey and David Pellauer (Chicago: University of Chicago Press, 1988), p. 187; (in French) *Temps et récit*, vol. 3 (Paris: Editions du Seuil, 1985), p. 273.

21. André Glucksmann, "La Considération de l'inhumain," in Mario Bettati and Bernard Kouchner, *Le Devoir d'ingérence* (Paris: DeNoël, 1987), p. 218.

22. Lévinas, *La Souffrance inutile*, p. 114.

23. Milan Kundera, *Testaments Betrayed*, trans. Linda Asher (New York: HarperCollins, 1995), p. 240; (in French) *Les Testaments trahis* (Paris: Gallimard, 1993), p. 279.

24. Rony Brauman, *Humanitaire: Le Dilemme: Entretien avec Philippe Petit* (Paris: Textuel, 1996), p. 35.

25. Ibid.

chapter six Of Angels and Men

1. Henri Michaux, *Face aux verrous* (Paris: Gallimard, coll. "Poésie," 1992), p. 77.

2. Meg Greenfield, "Intervention Fatigue," in a special column, "The Last Word," *Newsweek*, October 25, 1993, p. 80.

3. When I finished this translation in June 1999, NATO and Russia, with the endorsement of the U.N., had just negotiated a new peace settlement with Yugoslavia, this time to end the war in Kosovo and make it possible for one mil-

lion Albanian Kosovar refugees to return home after nearly three months of devastating ethnic cleansing and destruction. (J. Friedlander).

4. Pierre Bourdieu, *Le Désir d'Europe* (Paris: La Différence, 1992), p. 54.

5. Julien Benda, *Discours à la nation européenne* (Paris: Gallimard, coll. "Folio essais," 1992), p. 71.

6. Ibid., p. 125.

7. Ibid., pp. 126–27.

8. Hannah Arendt, " We Refugees," in Hannah Arendt, *Jew as Pariah* (New York: Grove Press, 1978), p. 55. First published in *The Menorah Journal*, January 1943, p. 69.

9. Jean Améry, *Par-delà le crime et le châtiment: Essais pour surmonter l'insurmontable* (Paris: Actes Sud, 1995), p. 85.

10. Ibid., p. 84.

11. Ibid.

12. Ibid., p. 85.

13. Ibid., p. 105.

14. Ibid., p. 99.

15. Albert O. Hirschman, *Défection et prise de parole* (Paris: Fayard, 1995), p. 175.

16. Hannah Arendt, *L'Impérialisme* (Paris: Fayard, 1982), p. 287.

17. Améry, *Par-delà le crime et le châtiment*, p. 96.

18. Ibid., p. 88.

19. Ibid., p. 92.

20. Ibid.

21. Ibid., p. 89.

22. Ibid., p. 88.

23. Emmanuel Lévinas, "Quelques réflexions sur la philosophie de l'hitlérisme," in *Cahier de l'Herne: Emmanuel Lévinas* (Paris: Le Livre de poche, coll. "Biblio essais," 1991), p. 118.

24. Mario Vargas Losa, "Cher Régis, tu sais aussi bien que moi . . .," *Libération*, December 2, 1993.

25. Nicholas Negroponte, *being digital* (New York: Knopf, 1995), p. 7.

26. Ibid., p. 198.

27. Chateaubriand, *Les Mémoires d'outre-tombe*, vol. 3 (Paris: Flammarion, 1982), pp. 587–88.

28. Michel Serres, *The Troubadour of Knowledge*, trans. Sheila Faria Glaser with William Paulson (Ann Arbor: University of Michigan Press, 1997), p. 147; (in French) *Le Tiers-Instruit* (Paris: François Bourin, 1991), p. 224.

29. Améry, *Par-delà le crime et le châtiment*, p. 103.

30. Gilbert K. Chesterton, *Heretics* (New York: John Lane, 1905), p. 49.

31. Pierre Nora, "Comment écrire l'histoire de France?" in *Les Lieux de mémoire*, vol. 3, part 1 (Paris: Gallimard, 1992), p. 30; (in English) *Realms of Memory: Rethinking the French Past*, vols. 1–3, ed. with a foreword by Lawrence D. Kritzman, trans. Arthur Goldhammer (New York: Columbia University Press, 1998) (chapter not translated in English ed.).

32. Hannah Arendt, *Men in Dark Times* (New York: Harcourt Brace & World, Inc., 1968), p. 25.

Epilogue

1. From the context it is clear that Hannah Arendt was referring to Nietzsche's concept of *ressentiment*, even if the English edition of her work does not keep the French spelling of resentment. Nietzsche used the French rendering of the word to remind the reader that he had given the term a specific philosophical meaning. (J. Friedlander).

2. Hannah Arendt, *The Burden of Our Time* (London: Secker and Warburg, 1951), p. 438.

3. Ibid., pp. 438–39.

index